# ABSOLUTELY CRAZY KNOWLEDGE

## The World's Funniest Collection of Amazing Facts

written by
**Christian Millman**

ACK Headmaster illustrations by
**Uijung Kim**

designed by
**Keith Plechaty**

**studio** fun BOOKS

White Plains, New York • Montréal, Québec • Bath, United Kingdom

Library of Congress Cataloging-in-Publication Data

Millman, Christian.
  Absolutely crazy knowledge : the world's funniest collection of amazing
facts : laugh your way to total brilliance! / by Christian Millman.
      pages cm
  ISBN 978-0-7944-3341-3 (alk. paper)
1. Curiosities and wonders. 2. Children's questions and answers. I.
Title.
  AG243.M53 2015
  031.02—dc23

All photos and art are copyright © Shutterstock.
Pages 6, 71: car/arosoft; page 13: Hollywood sign/Andrey Bayda; page 27:
Switzerland scene/Maisna; page 41: Isaac Newton/Nicku; page 42: orchestra/
Pavel L Photo and Video; page 43: choir/Ferenc Szelepcsenyi; page 44:
tank/OlegDoroshin; page 67: rocket/Jorg Hackemann; page 109: jumper in
wingsuit/Evgeniya Moroz; page 144: Rubik's Cube/Popartic

Published by Studio Fun International, Inc.
44 South Broadway, White Plains, NY 10601 U.S.A. and
Studio Fun International Limited,
The Ice House, 124-126 Walcot Street, Bath UK BA1 5BG
Printed in China.
Conforms to ASTM F963 and EN71
10 9 8 7 6 5 4 3 2 1    LPP/09/14

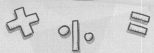

Dear Courageous Quiz Taker:

A hearty welcome to the *Absolutely Crazy Knowledge* test program, or, as we affectionately call it, the ACK Exams! After much research, we have determined that there is a better way to learn cool stuff. The answer: make it funny. You must believe this, too, as you are now holding this work of comic genius in your hands. May your life be transformed, and your future Nobel Prize guaranteed!

What lies before you is the challenge of ACK: eight quizzes that reveal your knowledge of all things that matter (that is, if what matters is strange science, freaky history facts, bizarre truths about your body, nutty stuff that happens in space, and the odd ways of artists and musicians).

Each quiz starts with lots of multiple-choice questions. Answers and explanations to each question are to be found one page-turn away. Each exam then concludes with rapid-fire True-False questions; answers to these are found on pages 148-150. You have your choice of test-taking methods:

1. You can read questions and then immediately look up the answers on the next spread. This method provides instant entertainment and learning, but also prevents any measurement of your ACK prowess. This might be a good thing.

2. You can read questions, write down answers on the answer sheets provided at back, and then score yourself later. Use this method to prove once and for all that your brain is thoroughly (fill in the blank).

3. Or, you can choose the path that I have taken, which is to put the burden of brilliance onto others. Hand out answer sheets to parents, brothers, sisters, or friends, and take ACK exams together!

As your ACK Headmaster, I am proud of you for taking on this epic and heroic challenge. We promise: The facts and fun you are about to encounter are unlike any you've seen before! We're sure you'll end up showing an ACK exam to your teacher so they can see how cool learning could be, if only they were more like ME.

Now on to ACK! Steel your mind, focus your attention, and, of course, make sure you visit the bathroom before starting, because it's an interruption to everyone around you when you start fidgeting in your seat because you forgot to take care of number one.

Good luck. Laugh. Learn.

Headmaster Charles Jimmy Bradley Hogg III

B.Sc., M.Ed., Ph.D., Litt.M., and Certified Yodeling Expert

# CONTENTS

# ACK EXAM 6

## NATURE

### Answer the Call of the Wild

Ever since humans lived in caves, we have wanted to know more about nature. For good reason--it can eat you! Here's how to learn without becoming some creature's lunch.

# ACK EXAM 7

## HISTORY

### Why Does It Repeat Itself? We said, WHY Does It Repeat Itself?

You may think of history as a bunch of dusty old people doing dusty old things. But remove the dust, and history is just old. But fun. Really. You'll see.

# ACK EXAM 8

## FUN AND GAMES

Do You Really Know How to Play? Hmmm, end the day with a math test, or a test about fun and games? Math or fun? Math? Fun? It's really hard to decide. Let's flip a coin...

# TRUE-FALSE ANSWERS

For each True-False section, you'll need to go to the back of the book for the answers. Sorry. We tried to fit them in a more convenient place, but the school bell rang, and we completely forgot about the whole thing.

# ANSWER SHEETS

Want to REALLY TRULY take the ACK Exams? Or, better, make your family take them? Then remove these blank answer sheets, grab your no. 2 pencils, and start answering!

# MULTIPLE CHOICE ANSWER KEY

Use this overlay to score your ACK Exams answer sheet.

## About the Author

If you want to say thanks for all the cool info and great laughs in this book, you should know its writer was Christian Millman. If you want to throw chewed gum wads at someone after reading it, it was written by his younger brother, Luke Millman. Because what's the point of a younger brother if you can't blame him for stuff? Christian lives and writes in a 150-year-old house in Nova Scotia that is also home to a small dog, a large cat, a son, a wife, and a friendly ghost named Mrs. Murphy. Christian has written for many magazines your parents probably read, and has co-authored many books, but none as awesome as this one.

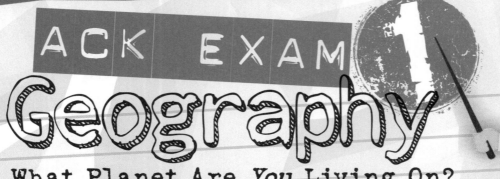

# ACK EXAM 1

# Geography

## What Planet Are *You* Living On?

**1** For the six movies that make up *The Hobbit* and *The Lord of the Rings* trilogies, the mythical land of Middle Earth was filmed entirely in which country?

**A.** Switzerland. You can tell from all the scenes with snowy mountains and orcs eating Swiss cheese.

**B.** New Zealand. Because New Zealand is where the last remaining elf tribes live, and they refuse to get on airplanes.

**C.** Spain. The name of the hobbit Bilbo Baggins is actually taken from Bilbao, a city in the Spanish province of Biscay where it was filmed.

**D.** StudioLand. They're movies. It's all computers, cardboard, and actors standing in front of screens.

**2** Seventy percent of Earth's surface is covered by water. How much of that is fresh water?

**A.** 2.5 percent. Better start taking shorter showers!

**B.** 10 percent. That includes rivers, lakes, and millions of tiny ponds made up of spilled drinks.

**C.** 30 percent. If 30 percent of Earth's surface is land, then 30 percent of the water should be land water, right?

**D.** 100 percent. It's all fresh water—whoever heard of stale water? Duh.

Answers on page 11

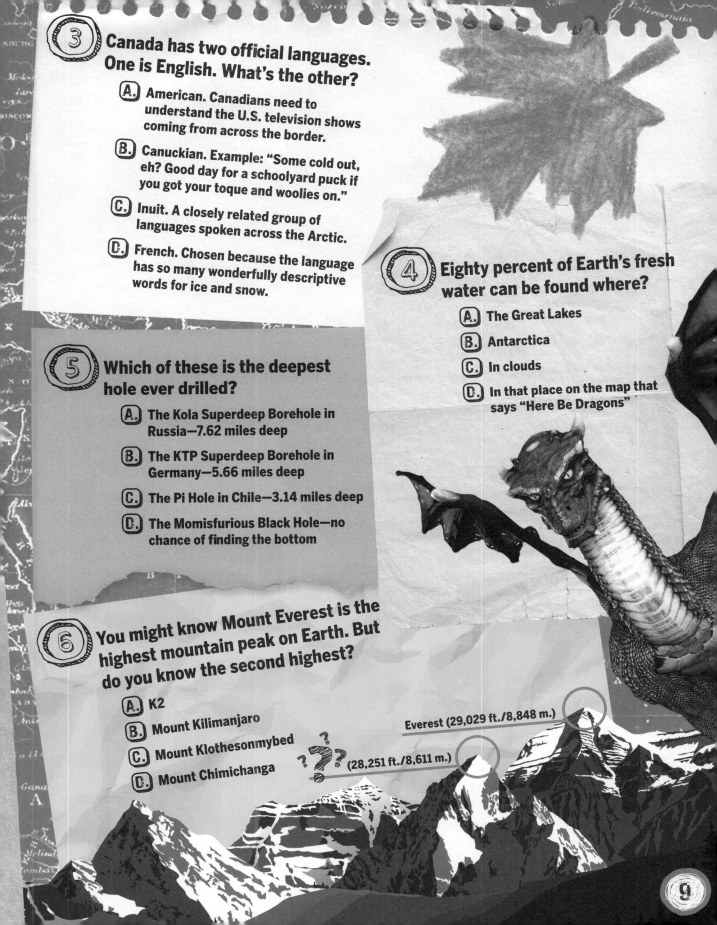

**3** Canada has two official languages. One is English. What's the other?

**A.** American. Canadians need to understand the U.S. television shows coming from across the border.

**B.** Canuckian. Example: "Some cold out, eh? Good day for a schoolyard puck if you got your toque and woolies on."

**C.** Inuit. A closely related group of languages spoken across the Arctic.

**D.** French. Chosen because the language has so many wonderfully descriptive words for ice and snow.

**4** Eighty percent of Earth's fresh water can be found where?

**A.** The Great Lakes

**B.** Antarctica

**C.** In clouds

**D.** In that place on the map that says "Here Be Dragons"

**5** Which of these is the deepest hole ever drilled?

**A.** The Kola Superdeep Borehole in Russia—7.62 miles deep

**B.** The KTP Superdeep Borehole in Germany—5.66 miles deep

**C.** The Pi Hole in Chile—3.14 miles deep

**D.** The Momisfurious Black Hole—no chance of finding the bottom

**6** You might know Mount Everest is the highest mountain peak on Earth. But do you know the second highest?

**A.** K2

**B.** Mount Kilimanjaro

**C.** Mount Klothesonmybed

**D.** Mount Chimichanga

Everest (29,029 ft./8,848 m.)

(28,251 ft./8,611 m.)

# Geography

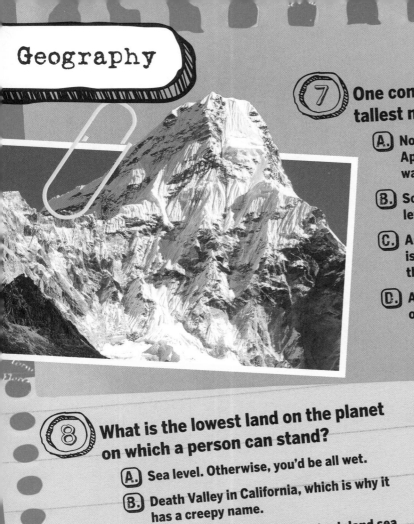

**7** One continent holds all 100 of the world's tallest mountains. Which continent is it?

- **A.** North America. Home to the Rockies and the Appalachians, there's barely room for amber waves of grain.
- **B.** South America. Look at a map, and the whole left side is filled with tall mountains.
- **C.** Asia. It's got to be Asia, because Mount Everest is there. Wait, Everest is in Alaska, right? Or is that Africa? Maybe it's Switzerland.
- **D.** All of the above. There are big mountains all over the planet. Question has to be wrong.

**8** What is the lowest land on the planet on which a person can stand?

- **A.** Sea level. Otherwise, you'd be all wet.
- **B.** Death Valley in California, which is why it has a creepy name.
- **C.** The shores of the Dead Sea (an inland sea between Israel and Jordan).
- **D.** The basement of the Empire State Building in New York City, allowing the building to claim it was both the lowest and highest spot on Earth when it was completed in 1931.

**9** Which country has the most land area?

- **A.** Russia
- **B.** Hong Kong (if you count the sides of its skyscrapers)
- **C.** Canada
- **D.** China

**10** Which spot on Earth is closest to the Moon?

- **A.** On top of Mount Everest. It's the tallest mountain, remember?
- **B.** On top of Mount Chimborazo
- **C.** On top of spaghetti, all covered in cheese
- **D.** China

Answers on page 13

## 11. What was the hottest day temperature ever recorded on Earth?

- **A.** 155°F, recorded at Flaming Mountain, China
- **B.** 134°F, in Death Valley, California
- **C.** 136°F, in El Aziziya, Libya
- **D.** 212°F, when my dad boiled over at seeing a scratch on his new car

## 12. How many countries make up the continent of Europe?

- **A.** There are 47 countries in Europe. Just don't ask me to name them.
- **B.** Trick question! Europe is a country, not a continent.
- **C.** 6. Germany, Great Britain, France, Ireland, Spain, and a funny one that looks like a boot.
- **D.** 30. Absolutely. For certain.

## 13. Lesotho, Vatican City, and San Marino have this trait in common:

- **A.** You have no idea where or what they are.
- **B.** The mascot for each one's national soccer team is a small horse named Mule Kick.
- **C.** They are the only cities in the world ruled by monarchs who each believe they are alien ambassadors to the citizens of Earth.
- **D.** They are the only countries in the world surrounded by a larger country on all sides.

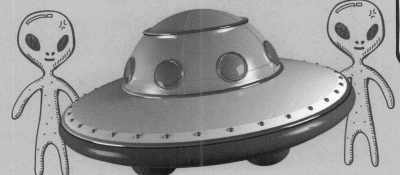

# Answers
### From pages 8-9

1. **B.** Peter Jackson, director of the movies, is from New Zealand and he chose his home nation to portray the beauty of Middle Earth. Scenes were filmed at more than 150 locations on the small island nation.

2. **A.** More than 97 percent of Earth's water is undrinkable salt water that makes up the planet's five oceans, plus many of its seas and lakes.

3. **D.** One-fifth of Canadians speak French as their mother tongue. All federal government services are available in both English and French.

4. **B.** The majority of the world's fresh water is locked in the ice sitting over the continent of Antarctica, or floating in icebergs near its shores.

5. **A.** Drilled for scientific research, the Kola Borehole in northwest Russia near Finland is full of surprises—including striking a deposit of hydrogen so massive it made mud coming from the hole "boil" with the gas.

6. **A.** Its name is boring, but not its elevation: At 28,251 feet, the peak of K2, a mountain on the Pakistan/China border, is only 778 feet lower than Mount Everest.

# Geography

Answers on page 15

**14** The shortest name for an actual geographic place is:

**A.** Yt. A village on the edge of the Sahara Desert, where centuries of heat and dryness have made vowels extremely scarce.

**B.** Å . It may be one letter, but do you know how to say it, smartypants?

**C.** Uh. A town in South Australia, so-called because nobody could remember the original name, Ozenkadnook.

**D.** Zed. A small city in Florida, named after the way its many British-born residents pronounce the last letter in the alphabet.

**15** Robinson Crusoe Island, named after a famed literary character, is an island belonging to which nation?

**A.** Deepsleepia

**B.** Great Britain, of course, because that's where Daniel Defoe, the author of Crusoe's adventure, is from.

**C.** How can an island belong to anyone? Silly question.

**D.** Chile

**16** China, India, and the United States are, in that order, the three largest countries in the world, based on population. Which country comes next?

**A.** Brazil

**B.** Antarctica (but only if you count penguins)

**C.** Indonesia

**D.** Birdland. You didn't say "human population," did you?

**17** Babylon was one of the greatest cities of ancient times. Which modern country would it lie in if it still existed?

- **A.** Israel
- **B.** Toysrusiskhan, perfectly preserved in plastic shrink wrap
- **C.** Hollywood, most recently seen in the film *The Hanging Garden*
- **D.** Iraq

 **18** The land for this U.S. state was purchased from Russia. Which one is it?

- **A.** Alaska. Even the Russians thought the climate was too cold.
- **B.** Massachusetts, the name for which comes from the Russian term for "clam chowder."
- **C.** The U.S. never bought land from Russia. That's crazy talk.
- **D.** Greenland. But the U.S. returned the land 10 years later after a Supreme Court challenge.

 **19** With almost 1.4 billion people, China is the world's largest country, by population. It also is home to the most populated city in the world. What is that city's name?

- **A.** Beijing. China's capital city is also its largest.
- **B.** Shanghai. Although its name was once synonymous with kidnapping, Shanghai is now better known for being the world's largest city.
- **C.** China. When its population passed one billion in the early 1980s, China became both a city and a country as all its regions were forced to squeeze together more tightly.
- **D.** Great Wall. Once a colony of Britain, this enormous city is so large it can be seen from space.

## Answers
### From pages 10-11

7. **C.** Mount Everest and the other 99 tallest mountains are all along a U-shaped span of mountain ranges in central and southern Asia. Each one is over 23,000 feet tall.

8. **C.** The surface of the Dead Sea is in a deep basin that is actually 427 meters (or 1,401 feet) below sea level.

9. **A.** Russia is, by far, the largest country in the world by land area, with over 6.3 million square miles. Next comes China, with 3.7 million square miles. The United States has just slightly more land than Canada; both are around 3.5 million square miles.

10. **B.** Yes, Mount Everest is the world's tallest when measured from bottom to top. But Mount Chimborazo, in the South American country of Ecuador, sits on a huge bulge in the Earth's crust, which pushes its peak closest to the moon.

11. **B.** Although C was, until recently, considered correct: El Aziziya, a desert location in northern Africa, recorded a temperature of 136°F in 1922. But, in 2012, a panel of scientists concluded the El Aziziya reading had to be in error, and gave the title of hottest place on earth back to Death Valley!

12. **A.** At the moment, Europe has 47 countries. But you might want to check again next week. The number has jumped in recent decades due to the breakups of the Soviet Union and Yugoslavia into many freestanding countries, and there are still a number of disputed borders and potential new nations.

13. **D.** Lesotho, a country of two million people, is completely located within the borders of South Africa. Vatican City, home of the Pope and the Catholic Church, is enclosed within the much larger city of Rome. San Marino, a country of just 30,000 people, sits like a small island in the mountains of northeastern Italy.

# Geography

Do you speak English?

**20** This flag belongs to which of the following nations?

A. China and Russia. These neighbors share a border and a flag.

B. McDonald's. The world's largest country, if measured by burger consumption.

C. Japan. The red and white give it away.

D. Indonesia and Monaco. They share it, as their citizens so like to visit each other's country.

**21** How many countries use English as an official language?

A. 1. Only the English speak English. Thou who attempt to speaketh English with such coarseness and imprecision insult the queen by suggesting that their utterances are of the same language as of her noble empire.

B. 56. Including Kiribati, Malawi, and Saint Lucia.

C. 3. England, the U.S., and Australia.

D. 196. You can speak English in all countries. After all, it's a free world.

**22** The Great Barrier Reef is the world's largest reef system. Where is it?

A. On Australia's northeast coast.

B. One mile off the coast of Treasure Island. It protects the island's vast riches, all buried by the legendary pirate Blackbeard.

C. It makes up the ice shelf surrounding Antarctica, and is patrolled by heavily armed emperor penguins.

D. Along the southeast coast of Florida, where it is visited by thousands of snorkelers every year.

Answers on page 17

**23** Lake Baikal is the deepest lake in the world, with a maximum depth of 5,369 feet. Where is it?

**A.** Russia, where it once had a temporary railroad on its frozen surface.

**B.** Zimbabwe, a country in southern Africa.

**C.** Caynine, a South American country. Dogs were first domesticated near Lake Baikal, the name of which represents the barking sound early canines made.

**D.** The center of the island of Fiji. The lake is so deep, it actually has no bottom; it just goes straight through to the ocean. Which is why in French, Fiji translates to "doughnut."

**24** Even though it's an island in the Pacific, Guam doesn't have any natural sand to mix into asphalt to make its roads. So it uses this material instead.

**A.** Gum. The roads look like the underside of a school desk, but they smell nice on hot days.

**B.** Coral

**C.** Shredded coconut

**D.** Fish scales

**25** Uganda, in central Africa, has the youngest median age in the world. How old would you say that is?

**A.** What does median age mean again? Is that the same as average age?

**B.** 72. People are living longer and longer these days.

**C.** 37. Some old, some young, it all evens out.

**D.** 15. Harsh conditions and a violent history add up to a tragically short average life span here.

## Answers
### From pages 12-13

14. **B.** In Sweden, there are at least eight villages that go by the name Å, and plenty more in Norway and Denmark. In these Scandinavian languages, Å means "small river."

15. **D.** Robinson Crusoe Island is situated in the Pacific Ocean off the coast of Chile, which claims it as Chilean soil.

16. **C.** Indonesia is the world's fourth most populous nation with more than 230 million citizens, followed by Brazil, which has about 193 million.

17. **C.** Babylon is now mostly dust, but its few remains lay roughly 85 kilometers (53 miles) south of Baghdad, the capital city of Iraq.

18. **A.** In 1867, the U.S. government paid Russia about two cents per acre for all the land in what is now America's 49th state.

19. **B.** With more than 23 million people, Shanghai is the world's largest proper city. On many lists, Tokyo—Japan's capital city—is listed as world's largest, but that's only true if you include the metropolitan areas outside city limits.

**26** In the Southeast Asian country of Vietnam, two drinks are available free in restaurants. One is water. What is the other?

A. Coffee. Vietnamese coffee is legendary for its delicious taste.

B. Soy milk. Yes, made from soybeans.

C. Tea. People drink tea here like Westerners drink soda pop.

D. Coke or Pepsi. Restaurants provide it for free to lure in customers.

**27** Which country is the longest in the world from north to south?

A. Brazil. Not just famous for nuts, you know.

B. Baobab. That's why there's the saying, "Tall as the baobab tree."

C. Chile. Look at a map: it's as long, tall, and skinny as a basketball player.

D. Norte-Sur. Everyone who has taken Spanish knows that!

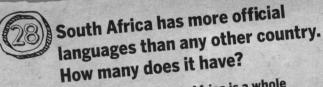

**28** South Africa has more official languages than any other country. How many does it have?

A. No fair! South Africa is a whole continent, isn't it? And who can guess the number of languages on a continent?

B. 11. How can South Africans possibly understand one another?

C. 2. English and Vuvuzela.

D. 1. But no one outside the country can pronounce its name.

Answers on page 19

**29** Which country produces the most amount of gold every year?

A. Moira. Dwarves dug mines here to harvest it all.

B. South Africa. There's more to the country than just diamonds, you know.

C. El Dorado. You know, that amazing place somewhere in South America.

D. China. This place positively glitters!

**30** Which of these places has the largest number of active volcanoes in the world?

A. Indonesia. Residents regularly have to outrun lava.

B. Iceland. They should call it Fireland instead.

C. The teacher's lounge. They're always blowing their tops in there.

D. Disney World, near Orlando, Florida. But don't worry, it's only a show, folks.

# Answers
## From pages 14-15

20. C. Yep, this is the national flag of both Indonesia and Monaco, the only two countries that have flags of the exact same design.

21. B. There are 56 countries using English as an official language. French is the second most common with about half that number.

22. A. Australia. The Great Barrier Reef, made up of more than 1,800 miles of living coral, is one of the natural wonders of the world.

23. A. Lake Baikal, in the Russian region of Siberia, is covered by thick ice for five months of the year.

24. B. Roads in Guam are made of an asphalt mix of coral and oil, which can make the roads really slippery when wet. That's why the island's speed limit on most roads is only 35mph.

25. C. Median age divides a population into two equal-size groups: older than that age, and younger than that age. In Uganda, it's only 15. Compare that to the United States, which has a median age of 37 years old.

Caldera

Lava

Volcanic Rock

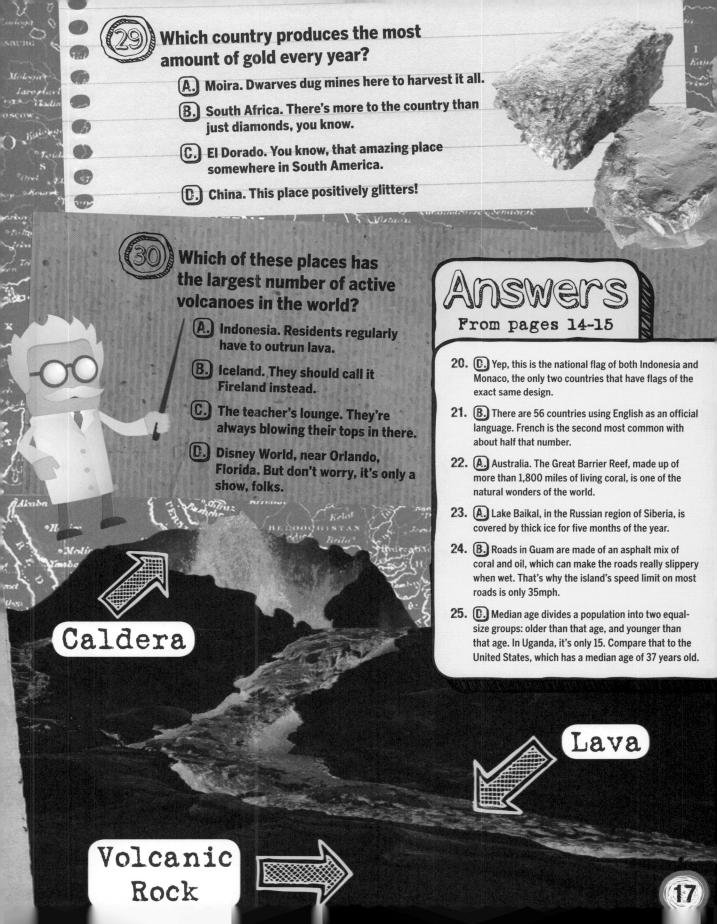

# Geography

**31** You've seen this symbol on maps. What's it called?

A. A pointer. Because it points. Obviously.

B. A captain's clock. Called this because sailors would rather know the direction than the time.

C. A tattoo design. Favored by rock stars who don't know up from down.

D. A compass rose. No, it doesn't smell like one.

**32** Greenland does not have enough what to play soccer?

A. Soccer players. Have you ever heard of a single soccer player from Greenland?

B. Flat spaces. The land is too broken up by mountains and chubby walruses.

C. Grass. So why do they call it Greenland?

D. Referees. Everyone wants to play, not run around in striped shirts and blow whistles.

**33** In the Central American country of Panama, you can use either of two official currencies. The first is the Panamanian balboa. What is the other?

A. The U.S. dollar. Surprisingly, George Washington bears a close resemblance to a popular Panamanian singer.

B. Hats. World-famous Panama hats are often used as currency due to their high value.

C. Canalis. Named for the Panama Canal and first used to pay workers who built it.

D. Corvina. An extremely popular and valuable fish in Panama, also used as currency, but you have to spend it quickly or it starts to smell.

Answers on page 21

**34** How many letters are in the longest place name on Earth?

**A.** 1,398,295. It takes almost four months to say the name.

**B.** 24. A little long, but most people can remember it with some practice.

**C.** 86. A real mouthful!

**D.** 1. But it's a very, very, very long letter.

**35** The United States leads the world in consumption of which precious resource?

**A.** Hot dogs. Especially when smothered in onions, mustard, and relish.

**B.** Oil. America is home of the brave and the giant SUV.

**C.** Football players. They work hard, play hard, and hurt hard.

**D.** Diamonds. But, boy, does the place ever sparkle.

## Answers
### From pages 16-17

26. **C.** You can get any of these drinks in Vietnam, but you'll pay for them—except tea. Either hot or iced, tea is available at no charge in almost all Vietnamese restaurants.

27. **A.** Brazil, in South America, covers more than 2,700 miles from north to south!

28. **B.** The 11 official languages of South Africa are English, Afrikaans, isiZulu, isiXhosa, Sesotho, Setswana, Sepedi, Xitsonga, siSwati, isiNdebele, and Tshivenda.

29. **D.** China extracts about 270 metric tons of gold from its mines every year. Australia, Russia, South Africa, and the United States are also large producers.

30. **A.** Indonesia has a staggering 127 active volcanoes, many of which erupt regularly.

**36** The Bahamas are a group of island in the Caribbean. How many islands are in that group?

**A.** 2. Just enough to make the Bahamas plural.

**B.** 700. Whaaattt? No way.

**C.** 123. Ba means the number one in the local language, ha means two, and ma means three. The name ba-ha-ma literally translates as 123, the number of islands in the chain.

**D.** Who knows? Isn't it enough to just sun on the beach and swim with the dolphins?

**37** Which country has been named the happiest in the world?

**A.** Christmas Island. Who can be unhappy with a name like that?

**B.** Japan. The people here live long and happy lives.

**C.** Djibouti. Mostly because it tickles when you say its name.

**D.** Norway. But it's because no one has told them they're living in Norway.

**38** Which country was named the saddest on the same scale?

**A.** Togo. Because it's sad to be named for takeout food.

**B.** Great Britain. That stiff upper lip hides a lot of unhappiness.

**C.** Taiwan. It's hard being China's little brother.

**D.** Australia. The kangaroos are hoppy, but the humans aren't happy.

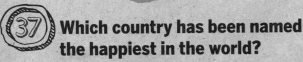

*Food to go*

Answers on page 23

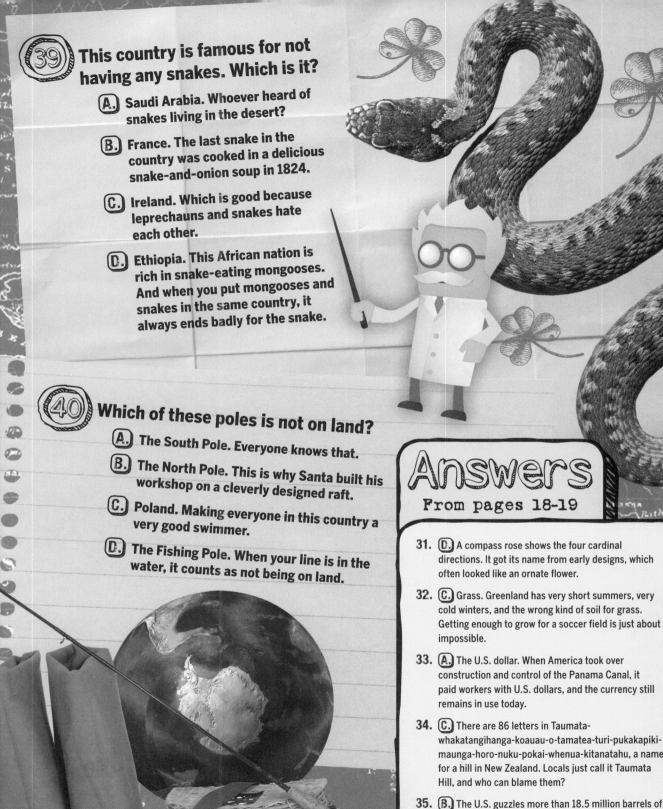

**39** This country is famous for not having any snakes. Which is it?

**A.** Saudi Arabia. Whoever heard of snakes living in the desert?

**B.** France. The last snake in the country was cooked in a delicious snake-and-onion soup in 1824.

**C.** Ireland. Which is good because leprechauns and snakes hate each other.

**D.** Ethiopia. This African nation is rich in snake-eating mongooses. And when you put mongooses and snakes in the same country, it always ends badly for the snake.

**40** Which of these poles is not on land?

**A.** The South Pole. Everyone knows that.

**B.** The North Pole. This is why Santa built his workshop on a cleverly designed raft.

**C.** Poland. Making everyone in this country a very good swimmer.

**D.** The Fishing Pole. When your line is in the water, it counts as not being on land.

## Answers
### From pages 18-19

31. **D.** A compass rose shows the four cardinal directions. It got its name from early designs, which often looked like an ornate flower.

32. **C.** Grass. Greenland has very short summers, very cold winters, and the wrong kind of soil for grass. Getting enough to grow for a soccer field is just about impossible.

33. **A.** The U.S. dollar. When America took over construction and control of the Panama Canal, it paid workers with U.S. dollars, and the currency still remains in use today.

34. **C.** There are 86 letters in Taumata-whakatangihanga-koauau-o-tamatea-turi-pukakapiki-maunga-horo-nuku-pokai-whenua-kitanatahu, a name for a hill in New Zealand. Locals just call it Taumata Hill, and who can blame them?

35. **B.** The U.S. guzzles more than 18.5 million barrels of oil per day. China, which has a population four times as large, uses 10.3 million barrels of oil per day.

# Geography

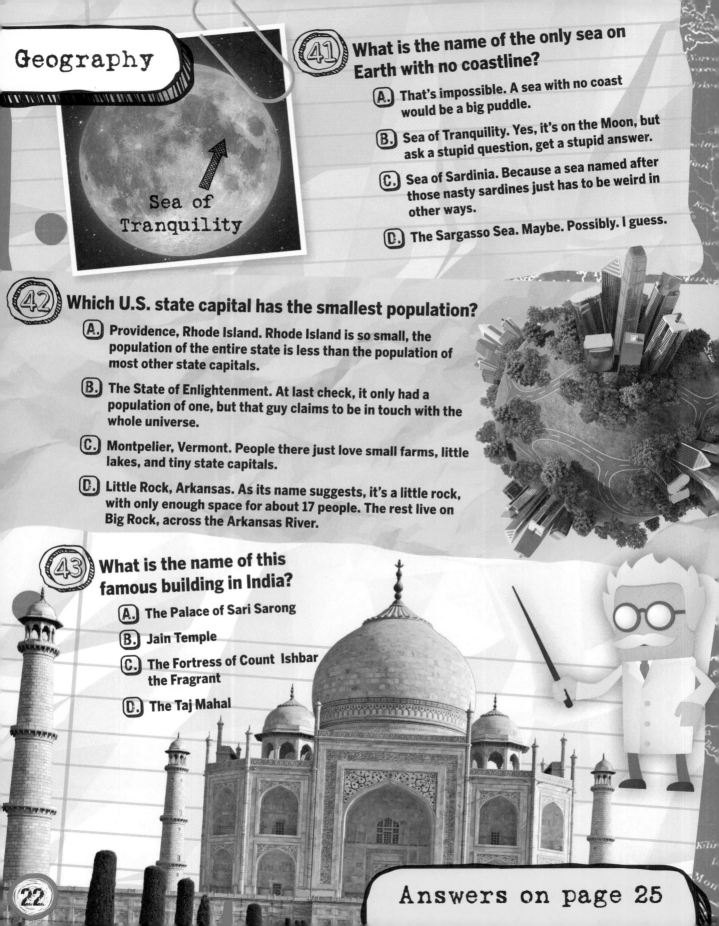

Sea of Tranquility

**41** What is the name of the only sea on Earth with no coastline?

A. That's impossible. A sea with no coast would be a big puddle.

B. Sea of Tranquility. Yes, it's on the Moon, but ask a stupid question, get a stupid answer.

C. Sea of Sardinia. Because a sea named after those nasty sardines just has to be weird in other ways.

D. The Sargasso Sea. Maybe. Possibly. I guess.

**42** Which U.S. state capital has the smallest population?

A. Providence, Rhode Island. Rhode Island is so small, the population of the entire state is less than the population of most other state capitals.

B. The State of Enlightenment. At last check, it only had a population of one, but that guy claims to be in touch with the whole universe.

C. Montpelier, Vermont. People there just love small farms, little lakes, and tiny state capitals.

D. Little Rock, Arkansas. As its name suggests, it's a little rock, with only enough space for about 17 people. The rest live on Big Rock, across the Arkansas River.

**43** What is the name of this famous building in India?

A. The Palace of Sari Sarong

B. Jain Temple

C. The Fortress of Count Ishbar the Fragrant

D. The Taj Mahal

Answers on page 25

## 44 Which of these rivers once reversed direction?

**A.** The Mississippi. That's why we learn to spell it backwards. ippississiM. See?

**B.** The Yangtze. China walled off so much of it for dams, the river's current had nowhere to go but back.

**C.** The River of Babylon. The event even made it into song lyrics.

**D.** The Amazon. In 1998, a logjam from extensive overharvesting of rain forests caused the river to reverse flow temporarily.

Yangtze

## 45 What is the distance around the earth at the Equator (its circumference)?

**A.** Earth is flat. It doesn't have a circumference.

**B.** 24,859 miles

**C.** 7,926 miles

**D.** It changes slightly from year to year when Mother Earth signs back up for weight-loss classes.

Equator

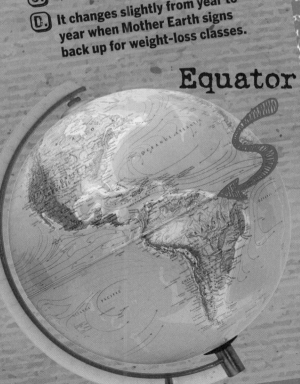

## Answers
### From pages 20-21

**36.** **B.** The Bahamas is made up of 700 individual islands, scattered over 100,000 square miles of sea.

**37.** **D.** Norway recently rated a 7.693 out of 10 on an international happiness scale, according to the United Nations. The U.S. scored 7.082 out of 10.

**38.** **A.** Togo, a small and impoverished country in northern Africa, rated only 2.936 out of 10 on the happiness scale.

**39.** **C.** According to legend, St. Patrick drove all the snakes out of Ireland. But scientists point to the cold climate and its island status. Note that Ireland does have snakes in some zoos and pet shops, just none in the wild.

**40.** **B.** The only thing you'll find at the North Pole is ice floating on top of a frigid ocean. The closest land is over 400 miles away.

**46** How many different north poles are used in navigation?

A. Oh, come on! Are you serious?

B. One. If you really are being serious, the answer is one. Now get that fever-induced delirium checked by a doctor.

C. Seriously. Are you serious?

D. Two. Just in case you're seeing double.

**47** This is an inukshuk. This particular style was used by the Inuit people of the Arctic to tell each other what?

A. You are on the right path.

B. Simon says, "Stand with your arms straight out."

C. It's so cold you need to start doing jumping jacks right now!

D. The Olympics are coming! The Olympics are coming!

**48** What is the world's longest river?

A. The Nile. To say otherwise is to be in De Nile. Ha!

B. The Mississippi. Tom Sawyer said so.

C. The Amazon. Or maybe that's the world's largest bookseller.

D. The London sewer system. Who knows how much flows below?

Answers on page 27

**49** **What is the International Date Line?**

**A.** It's where you go to meet people from other countries and then take them to dinner and a movie.

**B.** It's the line on Earth that Superman flew around fast enough to reverse time.

**C.** It's a world-famous cruise ship company.

**D.** It's where today becomes tomorrow.

**50** **If you made a deep enough hole in your backyard, where would you come out?**

**A.** The middle of the Pacific Ocean. I'm bringing my swimming trunks!

**B.** China. If my backyard were in Chile or Argentina, that is.

**C.** The yolk at the center of the planet would muck up my digging machine.

**D.** The place that's the opposite of heaven and that I'd rather not say out loud.

## Answers
### From pages 22-23

41. **D.** The Sargasso Sea floats in the middle of the North Atlantic Ocean but is not part of it. Its borders are created by four powerful currents, one on each side, that separate it from the rest of the Atlantic as they pass by.

42. **C.** Montpelier is home to only 8,000 residents, a population more typical for a medium-size university than a state capital.

43. **D.** It took 20,000 workers more than 22 years to build the Taj Mahal, which was completed in 1653.

44. **A.** Three massive earthquakes during the period of 1811-1822 actually caused the mighty Mississippi to flow backward for a time.

45. **B.** Earth's circumference at the Equator is almost 25,000 miles. Its diameter is 7,926 miles.

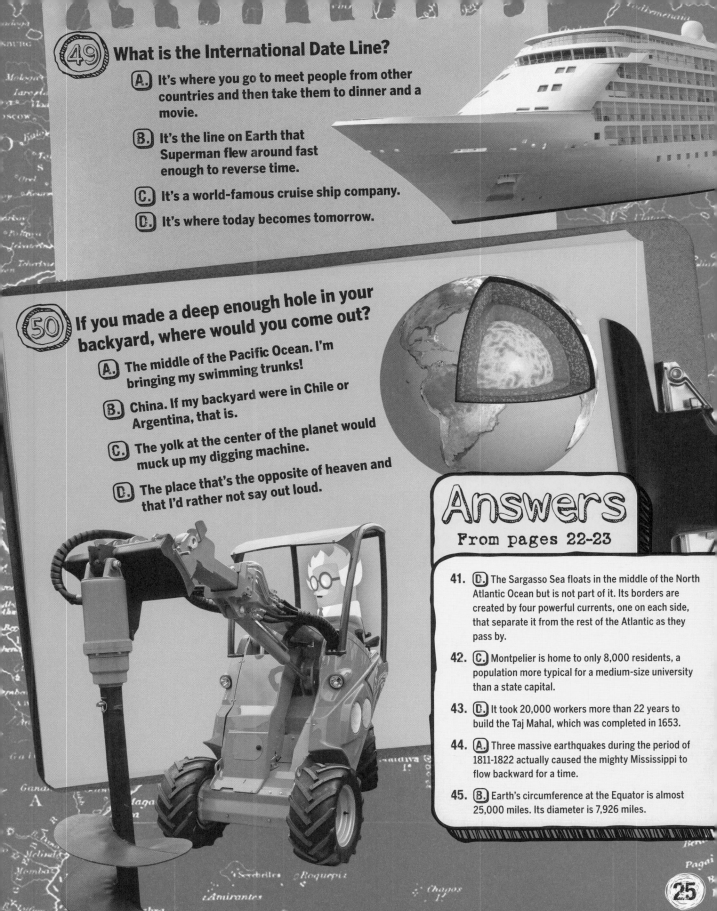

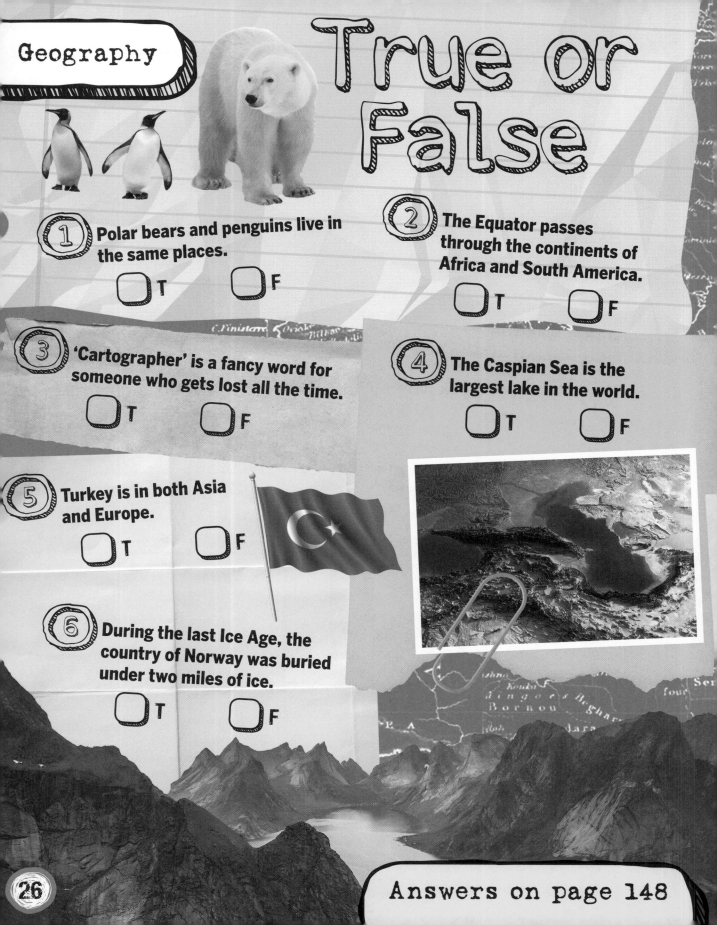

# Geography

# True or False

**1** Polar bears and penguins live in the same places.

☐ T     ☐ F

**2** The Equator passes through the continents of Africa and South America.

☐ T     ☐ F

**3** 'Cartographer' is a fancy word for someone who gets lost all the time.

☐ T     ☐ F

**4** The Caspian Sea is the largest lake in the world.

☐ T     ☐ F

**5** Turkey is in both Asia and Europe.

☐ T     ☐ F

**6** During the last Ice Age, the country of Norway was buried under two miles of ice.

☐ T     ☐ F

Answers on page 148

**7** Europe is the largest continent.

◻ T   ◻ F

**8** People from New Zealand hate it when you call them a Kiwi.

◻ T   ◻ F

**9** San Marino is the oldest country in the world.

◻ T   ◻ F

**10** Burgers and hot dogs were invented in Germany.

◻ T   ◻ F

**12** The term 'continental drift' refers to people who wander the planet aimlessly.

◻ T   ◻ F

**11** The official language of Switzerland is Swiss.

◻ T   ◻ F

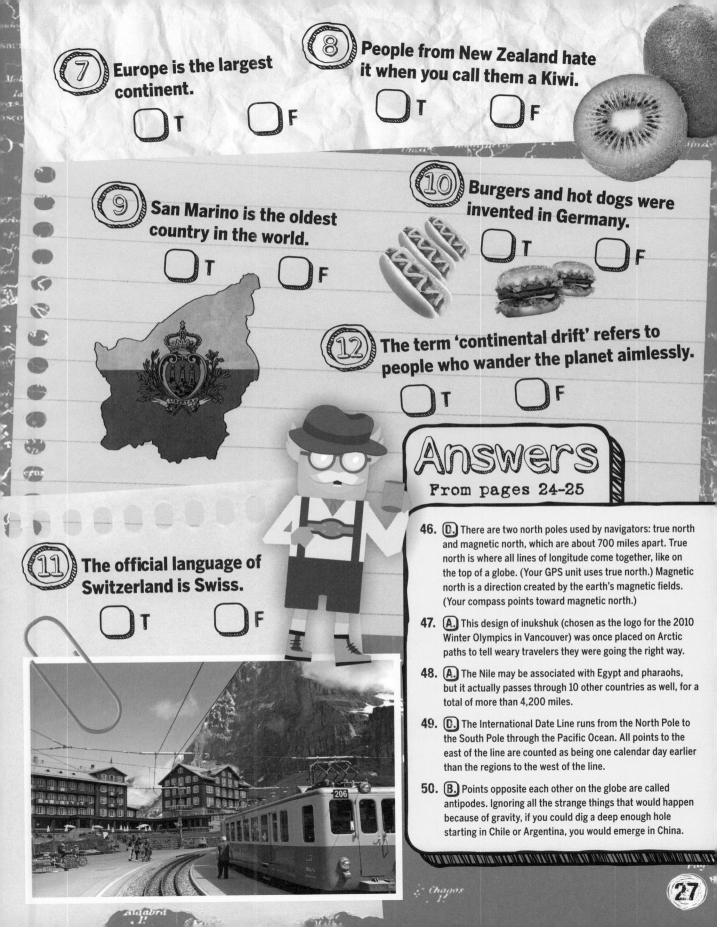

# Answers
### From pages 24-25

46. **D.** There are two north poles used by navigators: true north and magnetic north, which are about 700 miles apart. True north is where all lines of longitude come together, like on the top of a globe. (Your GPS unit uses true north.) Magnetic north is a direction created by the earth's magnetic fields. (Your compass points toward magnetic north.)

47. **A.** This design of inukshuk (chosen as the logo for the 2010 Winter Olympics in Vancouver) was once placed on Arctic paths to tell weary travelers they were going the right way.

48. **A.** The Nile may be associated with Egypt and pharaohs, but it actually passes through 10 other countries as well, for a total of more than 4,200 miles.

49. **C.** The International Date Line runs from the North Pole to the South Pole through the Pacific Ocean. All points to the east of the line are counted as being one calendar day earlier than the regions to the west of the line.

50. **B.** Points opposite each other on the globe are called antipodes. Ignoring all the strange things that would happen because of gravity, if you could dig a deep enough hole starting in Chile or Argentina, you would emerge in China.

# ACK EXAM 2

## Music
### In One Ear and Out the Other

**1** Which of these is the real definition of music?

- **A.** Anything that combines sound and rhythm to create beauty or emotion.
- **B.** Voices or instruments making nice sounds.
- **C.** Being told that school has been canceled.
- **D.** Hey, it's all about the groove. If you can't dance to it, how can you call it music?

**2** The famous composer Beethoven used to do what before he worked on a new piece of music?

- **A.** Text his mom and ask her to bake him chocolate chip cookies.
- **B.** Take off his shirt and pants and work in his Spiderman underwear.
- **C.** Pray for inspiration.
- **D.** Dip his head in cold water.

**3** Which of these is an actual song title?

- **A.** "I Don't Know Why, But My Stomach Makes Noises Whenever I Hug Someone"
- **B.** "21 Things That Make Me Say Ewwwww"
- **C.** "Regretting What I Said to You when You Called Me 11:00 on a Friday Morning to Tell Me that at 1:00 Friday Afternoon You're Gonna Leave Your Office, Go Downstairs, Hail a Cab to Go Out to the Airport to Catch a Plane to Go Skiing in the Alps for Two Weeks, Not that I Wanted to Go with You, I Wasn't Able to Leave Town, I'm Not a Very Good Skier, I Couldn't Expect You to Pay My Way, But after Going Out with You for Three Years I DON'T Like Surprises!!"
- **D.** "Happy Birthday, You Belong in a Zoo"

Answers on page 31

**4** Which of these is the world's best-selling musical instrument?

A. The nose bugle

A. The armpit squeeze

A. The ear horn

D. The mouth organ

**5** What is this?

A. Isn't that what comes out of cartoon characters' mouths when they say bad words?

B. It's a symbol on sheet music that means "stand up and take a bow."

C. It's a treble clef, a symbol used in sheet music that signals the pitch of each of the written notes.

D. It's what happens when you cook alphabet noodles too long.

**6** Which of these is unique to Japan's national anthem?

A. It's in Japanese. Come on, don't make the questions so easy.

B. It's only four lines long.

C. The full version has 158 verses, takes 90 minutes to perform, and almost no one can sing the whole thing.

D. It's sung to the same melody as "We Are the Champions" by the rock group Queen.

**7** What was the U.S. national anthem before 1931?

A. "The Star-Spangled Banner"

B. "My Country 'Tis of Thee"

C. There wasn't one because singing hadn't been invented yet.

D. "Old MacDonald Had a Farm"

**8** What is the world's most expensive musical instrument?

A. A saxophone played by jazz great Charlie Parker

B. A violin from the 1700s

C. The theremin Sheldon played on *The Big Bang Theory*

D. The piano Beethoven used to compose his nine symphonies

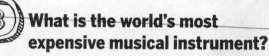

**9** What are the three main families of musical instruments?

A. Wait. Are you saying my clarinet has a family? Should I arrange a reunion?

B. The Weasleys, the Simpsons, and the Fantastic Four

C. Strings, percussion, and wind

D. Ancient, traditional, and modern

Answers on page 33

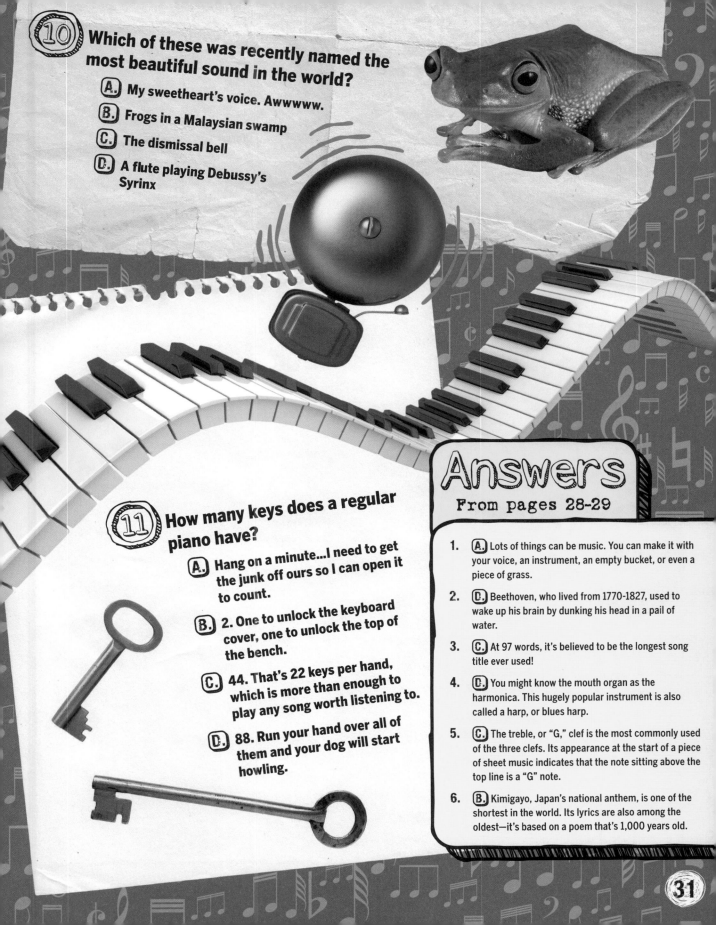

**10** Which of these was recently named the most beautiful sound in the world?

**A.** My sweetheart's voice. Awwwww.

**B.** Frogs in a Malaysian swamp

**C.** The dismissal bell

**D.** A flute playing Debussy's Syrinx

**11** How many keys does a regular piano have?

**A.** Hang on a minute...I need to get the junk off ours so I can open it to count.

**B.** 2. One to unlock the keyboard cover, one to unlock the top of the bench.

**C.** 44. That's 22 keys per hand, which is more than enough to play any song worth listening to.

**D.** 88. Run your hand over all of them and your dog will start howling.

## Answers

From pages 28-29

1. **A.** Lots of things can be music. You can make it with your voice, an instrument, an empty bucket, or even a piece of grass.

2. **D.** Beethoven, who lived from 1770-1827, used to wake up his brain by dunking his head in a pail of water.

3. **C.** At 97 words, it's believed to be the longest song title ever used!

4. **D.** You might know the mouth organ as the harmonica. This hugely popular instrument is also called a harp, or blues harp.

5. **C.** The treble, or "G," clef is the most commonly used of the three clefs. Its appearance at the start of a piece of sheet music indicates that the note sitting above the top line is a "G" note.

6. **B.** Kimigayo, Japan's national anthem, is one of the shortest in the world. Its lyrics are also among the oldest—it's based on a poem that's 1,000 years old.

**12** What is this person doing?

A. He's playing a didgeridoo.

B. He's using a blow dart gun, also called a blowgun.

C. He's drinking a thick milkshake through a really big straw.

D. He's playing a bassoon.

**13** None of the four members of The Beatles, one of the most famous rock bands of all time, could do what?

A. Read or write music

B. Play instruments other than the guitar and drums

C. Beat the members of the Rolling Stones in ping-pong

D. Remember the lyrics to the song "Happy Birthday to You"

**14** What happens to your houseplants if you play lots of music for them?

A. They start to lean toward the source of the sound.

B. Nothing. They're plants. They need WATER.

C. They grow faster.

D. They get tattoos, form a band, and sign a deal with a music producer who steals all their money.

Answers on page 35

**15** **Some opera singers can sing notes so high, this happens.**

- **A.** Dogs begin to howl.
- **B.** Earplug sales go up.
- **C.** Glass shatters.
- **D.** A small number of people faint.

**16** **What are these called?**

- **A.** They're called antiques.
- **B.** They must be some kind of radioactive disc because my parents say I'll die if I ever touch one of theirs.
- **C.** They're old CDs.
- **D.** They're records.

## Answers

### From pages 30-31

**7.** **B.** "My Country 'Tis of Thee" is actually sung to the same melody as "God Save the Queen," the British national anthem.

**8.** **B.** A violin made 300 years ago by Bartolomeo Giuseppe Antonio Guarnieri sold recently for $3.9 million.

**9.** **C.** This system of classifying instruments into three families dates back to ancient Greece.

**10.** **B.** The two-minute recording, called "Dusk by the Frog Pond," was judged "a symphony of life expressing itself."

**11.** **D.** A piano has an enormous range of sound, from a deep bassoon to a high piccolo.

**17** How old was the classical composer, Wolfgang Amadeus Mozart, when he wrote his first pieces of music?

**A.** 5 years old. His Teddy Bear Fugue has been played by orchestras ever since.

**B.** 18 years old. That's the minimum legal music-composing age where he lived.

**C.** 93 years old. He was a late bloomer. A really, really late bloomer.

**D.** Hey, that's my cat's name! He can't write music, but he purrs in different keys. Does that count?

MEOW

**18** One of the most famous and successful singers of all time was Elvis Presley. What was the one thing he never did?

**A.** Turn down a fried peanut butter and banana sandwich.

**B.** Reveal his real name, which was Slappy Apples.

**C.** Play the guitar.

**D.** Write his own songs.

Answers on page 37

## 19. When listening to quiet music in a quiet place, what usually happens to your body, if you are a typical person?

**A.** It gets bored. So does my brain. Booooooring.

**B.** My heartbeat slows down, my mind gets less busy, and my muscles relax. It's super nice.

**C.** My parents wonder what's wrong with me. They say things like "Who are you, and what have you done with our child?"

**D.** I get smarter. Math homework, anyone?

## 20. How fast is the speed of music?

**A.** If it's a good song, it's as fast as I can share it with friends.

**B.** If it's a lousy song, it's as slow as a new bottle of ketchup.

**C.** It's the same as the speed of sound. Music is sound, right?

**D.** It's the same as the speed of light. Music is light, right?

## Answers
### From pages 32-33

**12. A.** The didgeridoo, developed by ancient Aborigines in Australia, is the oldest known wind instrument.

**13. A.** In a 1980 interview, John Lennon said, "None of us can read music. None of us can write it." But could they ever make it!

**14. C.** No one knows why, but music tends to help plants grow faster and look healthier.

**15. C.** If an opera singer hits a note high enough and loud enough, it can cause nearby glass to vibrate and shatter.

**16. D.** Records were the main way people listened to music from the 1930s to the 1980s. A record has very narrow, pitted grooves; a stylus riding in the grooves translates the varying friction into sound.

# Music

**21** If you stood on the bottom of the ocean and sang a song, what would be the effect on your audience?

**A.** Have you completely lost your marbles? You have, haven't you?

**B.** First, they'd say, "Why are we standing on the ocean floor listening to this?" Then they'd swim up for air.

**C.** Water is denser than air, so it would take longer for my lovely song to reach them.

**D.** My song would reach them faster than it would above water.

**22** And if you stood in the middle of a giant block of iron and sang a song, what would be the effect on your audience?

**A.** OK, I'm seeing the principal. You've been writing tests about 50 years past your warranty.

**B.** First, they'd say, "Why are we in the middle of a block of metal? No song is worth that." Then they'd break out and go home.

**C.** Iron is crazy dense compared to air, so my song would get stuck.

**D.** My song would reach them even faster than through water.

Answers on page 39

## 23

**And if you stood in outer space and sang a song, what would be the effect on your audience?**

A. I don't know what to say. I feel sorry for you. Get help.

B. First, they'd say, "Why are we freezing our butts off in space? I hate this song." Then they'd head for Earth.

C. Space is way less dense than air, so they'd hear my song faster.

D. They wouldn't hear a thing.

## 24

**This type of musical instrument has been around for at least 12,000 years and is one of the earliest made by humans. What's it called?**

A. An ocarina, member of a family of instruments called vessel flutes.

B. Hey! That's the flute from The Legend of Zelda! I played it on my Xbox to get rid of the River Devil. Thanks, little flute!

C. A bugpipe. Later, larger versions were called a bagpipe.

D. A frog drum. So called because it makes croaking sounds when you rub a wet finger over the holes.

## Answers

### From pages 34-35

17. **A.** A musical prodigy, five-year-old Mozart composed several small pieces and played them for his father, who wrote them down.

18. **D.** Even though he was known as "The King of Rock and Roll," everything Elvis sang was written by other musicians.

19. **B.** Your body responds to soft music by slowing down and relaxing. It's a scientifically proven way to tune out any troubles or just chill for a while.

20. **C.** Music is sound, and sound travels through dry, warm air at a speed of 767 miles per hour.

Brrrrr

**25** Do you ever get chills or shivers when you listen to great music? Do you know why?

A. Because I like listening to music outdoors. In the winter. With no pants on. Brrrrr.

B. Because my body releases a feel-good substance.

C. The sound waves move the little hairs on my skin.

D. This doesn't happen to me! Bummer, because it sounds weirdly awesome.

**26** Who invented the compact disc, or CD?

A. Those old things? Benjamin Franklin invented them and he almost got electrocuted doing it.

B. A guy named Charlie Daniels. CDs are named after his initials.

C. Two electronics companies, Sony and Philips

D. Two toymakers, Mattel and Lego

**27** How do toilets contribute to the world of music?

A. Most of them flush in the note of E-flat.

B. I don't know about you, but I like to sing on mine.

C. For a brief moment, they drown out the sound of people playing the accordion.

D. Old ones can be recycled into piano keys.

Answers on page 41

**28** Birds and humans share this interesting musical ability.

**A.** Both can learn music before they're born.

**B.** Both agree that a screeching saxophone isn't really music at all.

**C.** Both instinctively head toward places where music is being played.

**D.** Both like to strut in silly ways while singing. (Proof: Mick Jagger is actually a bird.)

**29** If you ever have to have surgery, what should you tell the surgeon to do?

**A.** Wash his or her hands. Twice.

**B.** Finish medical school.

**C.** Choose his or her favorite music and play it during the surgery.

**D.** Sing show tunes while working on you.

## Answers

From pages 36-37

21. **D.** Sound moves through water four times faster than it does through air. Cool, huh?

22. **D.** Sound travels through iron about 15 times faster than it does through air. Fabuloso, no?

23. **D.** Sound needs to travel through something. Outer space is almost completely a vacuum where no sound can exist. Super groovy, eh?

24. **A.** Over the centuries, ocarinas have been made from bone, clay, wood, metal, and glass.

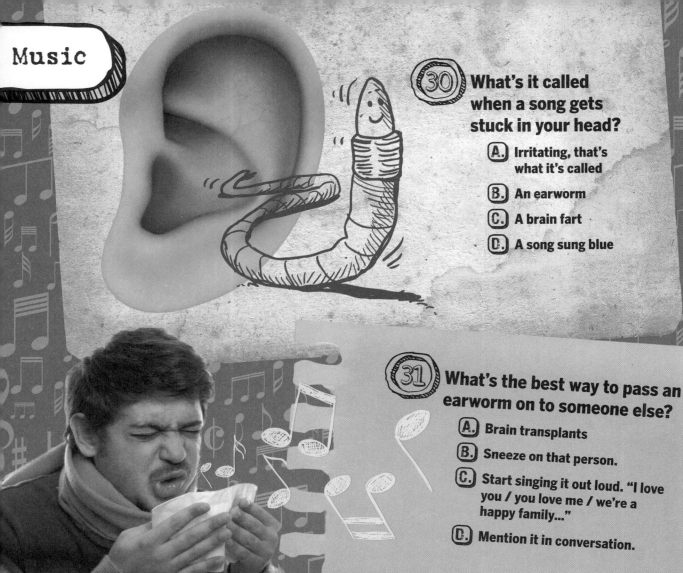

# Music

**30** What's it called when a song gets stuck in your head?

A. Irritating, that's what it's called

B. An earworm

C. A brain fart

D. A song sung blue

**31** What's the best way to pass an earworm on to someone else?

A. Brain transplants

B. Sneeze on that person.

C. Start singing it out loud. "I love you / you love me / we're a happy family..."

D. Mention it in conversation.

**32** What do 70 percent of adults wish they had done as kids?

A. Ran away from home and joined the circus.

B. Learned to play a musical instrument.

C. Learned to sing better.

D. Pursued a career as a professional sheet-music page turner.

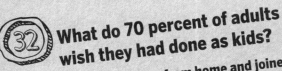

Answers on page 43

**33** The reason dancers tell each other to "break a leg" before a performance is...

A. They really don't like each other.

B. They're giving instructions on what to do to audience members who don't turn off their mobile phones.

C. They're wishing each other good luck.

D. They're recommending fellow dancers to eat more calcium-rich foods.

**34** Who said, "If I were not a physicist, I would probably be a musician"?

A. Albert Einstein

B. The lead singer of the punk band The Physicists.

C. Dr. Jekyll. But only when he wasn't being Mr. Hyde, because Mr. Hyde wanted to be an accountant.

D. Isaac Newton

## Answers
### From pages 38-39

25. **B.** It's called musical frisson. And it causes your body to release dopamine, a hormone that makes you feel good.

26. **C.** Philips and Sony had been working independently on the technology, but joined forces in the early 1980s to release the CD format still in use today.

27. **A.** It can vary, but most toilets flush in a perfect E-flat.

28. **A.** After they're born, both birds and babies can recognize songs they've heard before birth.

29. **C.** Research shows that surgeons who choose their own tunes and play them during surgery have better results for their patients.

# Music

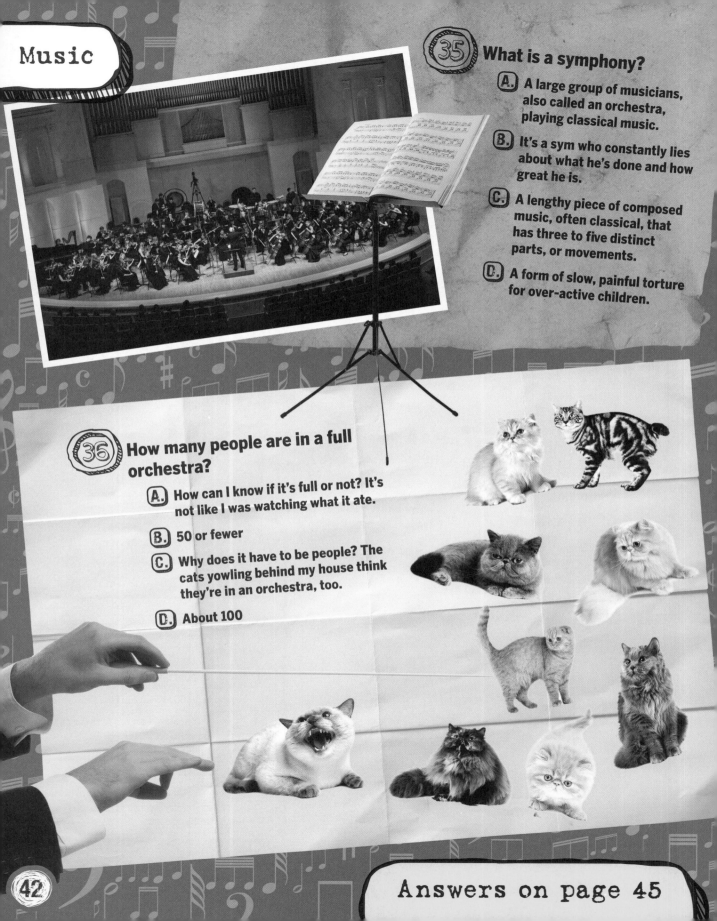

**35** **What is a symphony?**

**A.** A large group of musicians, also called an orchestra, playing classical music.

**B.** It's a sym who constantly lies about what he's done and how great he is.

**C.** A lengthy piece of composed music, often classical, that has three to five distinct parts, or movements.

**D.** A form of slow, painful torture for over-active children.

**36** **How many people are in a full orchestra?**

**A.** How can I know if it's full or not? It's not like I was watching what it ate.

**B.** 50 or fewer

**C.** Why does it have to be people? The cats yowling behind my house think they're in an orchestra, too.

**D.** About 100

Answers on page 45

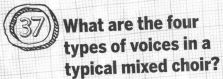

**37** **What are the four types of voices in a typical mixed choir?**

**A.** Guitar, piano, bass, and drums

**B.** Soprano, alto, tenor, and bass

**C.** Wynken, Blynken, Stynken, and Nod

**D.** Girls, boys, women, and men

**38** **What is jazz?**

**A.** Wow, that's really hard to answer. But I know it when I hear it.

**B.** It's a radio station my mom listens to when she's had a long day.

**C.** It's when surprised kittens throw their paws up by their faces and look super cute.

**D.** It's dance music played by people wearing suits or nice dresses.

## Answers

From pages 40–41

30. **B.** Once they're bouncing around in your head, earworms are hard to remove. One of the few ways to do that is to pass it on to someone else.

31. **C.** If some one hears you singing, there's a 9 in 10 chance that person will start singing the same song shortly.

32. **B.** Only 20 percent of kids actually learn to play an instrument. Those who don't go on to become adults who wish they had.

33. **C.** The dance world is known for its superstitions. Dancers believe it's bad luck to say "good luck," so they say the exact opposite.

34. **A.** Einstein also said, "I often think in music. I live my daydreams in music. I get most joy in life out of music."

# True or False

**1** Termites eat wood twice as fast if they hear heavy metal music.

☐ T  ☐ F

**2** Houseflies always buzz in the key of F major.

☐ T  ☐ F

**3** The national orchestra of Monaco is bigger than its military.

☐ T  ☐ F

**4** The longest piano composition ever takes six hours to play.

☐ T  ☐ F

**5** Some rappers can rap more than 10 syllables per second.

☐ T  ☐ F

Answers on page 148

**6** Trumpets have been around since at least 1500 B.C.

⬜ T ⬜ F

**7** Some whales can daze fish with a song.

⬜ T ⬜ F

**8** The guitar was invented in the United States.

⬜ T ⬜ F

**9** The largest disco dance was in Buffalo, New York, in 1979.

⬜ T ⬜ F

**10** A guy named Leo Fender invented the electric guitar.

⬜ T ⬜ F

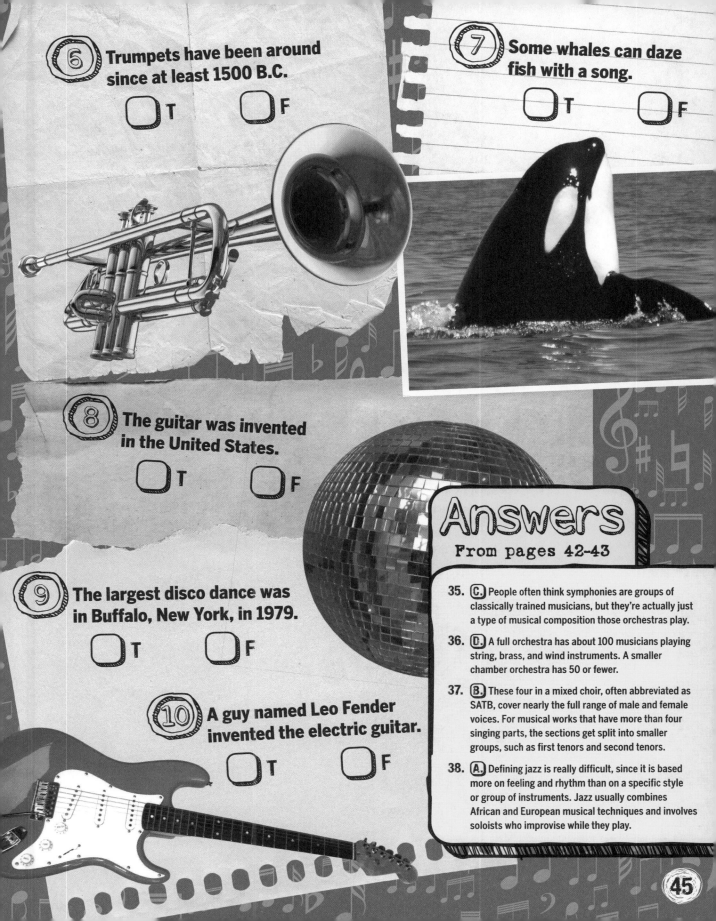

## Answers
### From pages 42-43

**35.** **C.** People often think symphonies are groups of classically trained musicians, but they're actually just a type of musical composition those orchestras play.

**36.** **D.** A full orchestra has about 100 musicians playing string, brass, and wind instruments. A smaller chamber orchestra has 50 or fewer.

**37.** **B.** These four in a mixed choir, often abbreviated as SATB, cover nearly the full range of male and female voices. For musical works that have more than four singing parts, the sections get split into smaller groups, such as first tenors and second tenors.

**38.** **A.** Defining jazz is really difficult, since it is based more on feeling and rhythm than on a specific style or group of instruments. Jazz usually combines African and European musical techniques and involves soloists who improvise while they play.

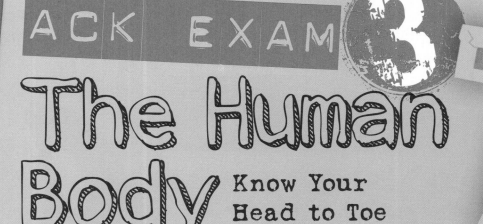

# The Human Body
### Know Your Head to Toe

1. **How fast can nerve signals travel to and from your brain?**

   A. Super slow before breakfast, super fast after a candy bar.

   B. Over 9,000! 9,000 of what, I don't know.

   C. Up to 35 miles per hour. Just like my grandma driving.

   D. Up to 200 miles per hour. Just like my dad driving.

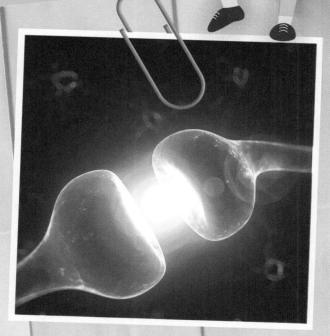

2. **How much spit will you produce in your lifetime?**

   A. Enough to fill two big buckets

   B. Enough to fill two bathtubs

   C. Enough to fill two swimming pools

   D. Enough to make my drooly dog really jealous

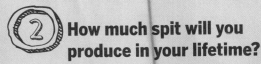

Answers on page 49

### 3 What is the strongest muscle in your body?

**A.** The gluteus maximus. Hey, wait! Isn't that my butt?

**B.** The quadriceps, also known as the thighs.

**C.** The tongue. I'm not sticking it out at you—I'm just exercising.

**D.** Whatever muscle keeps my supper in my stomach when I have to eat Brussels sprouts or spinach.

### 4 Which of these can people do?

**A.** Tickle themselves

**B.** Lick their elbows

**C.** Sneeze with their eyes open

**D.** All of the above

### 5 Where are the Islets of Langerhans located?

**A.** In the Black Sea, near the Russian border

**B.** In northern Canada, populated mostly by walruses

**C.** Along the coast of Chile. WHY is this question here, rather than on the geography test?

**D.** Sure, go ahead, tell me it's in some insane place like my pancreas. Whatever.

**6** **The term 'borborygmi' refers to what?**

A. The noise my stomach makes when I'm hungry

B. The noise my mouth makes when I'm hungry. It is pronounced: "I'M HUNGRY!"

C. The noise my lungs make when breathing with a chest cold

D. One freckle that looks different from others around it

**7** **How many muscles does a finger have?**

A. 5. Something about five sounds right.

B. This little piggy had none.

C. 9. You've got all kinds of bending and lifting capability in a finger. That takes muscles!

D. 23. I chose that because it's the biggest number here, and there are like a gazillion muscles in a body.

**8** **How much skin do humans shed?**

A. About 600,000 particles every hour.

B. Hey, we're not snakes! We don't shed our skin.

C. About 600,000 particles every year.

D. The same as a cat, except humans don't get as many hairballs.

Skin cells

Answers on page 51

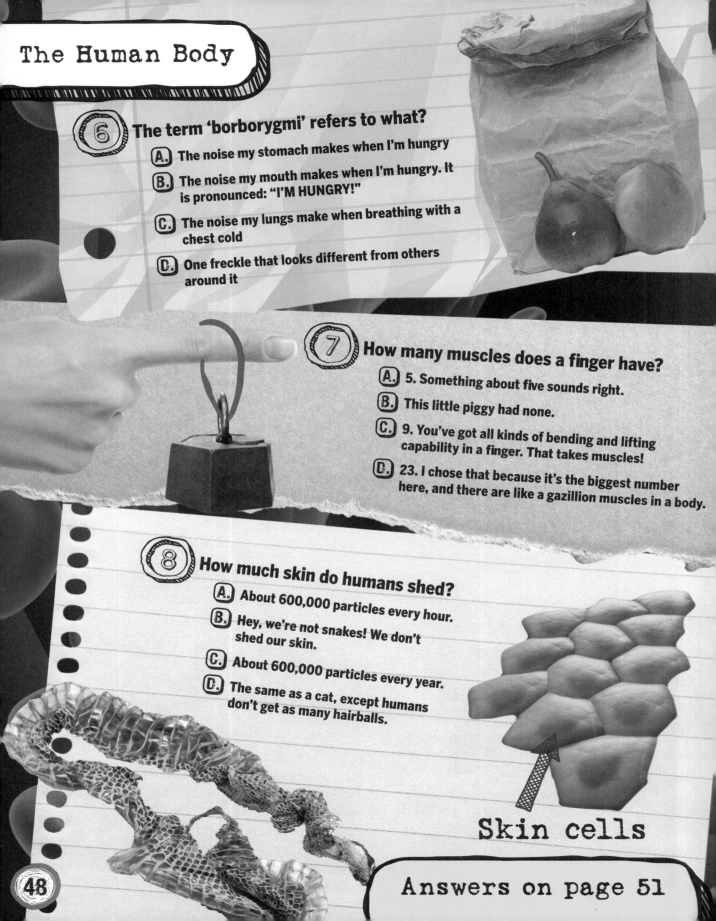

## 9. What do your tongue and fingertips have in common?

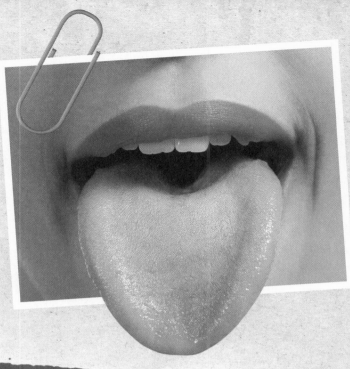

**A.** I put them both in the cookie dough.

**B.** I use both of them to make gestures I'm not supposed to.

**C.** They both leave unique prints on my bedroom window.

**D.** Both of them can be used to read braille.

## 10. Which of these can you NOT do when your nose is plugged?

**A.** Hum a tune

**B.** Sneeze

**C.** Taste food

**D.** Sound intelligent when you talk

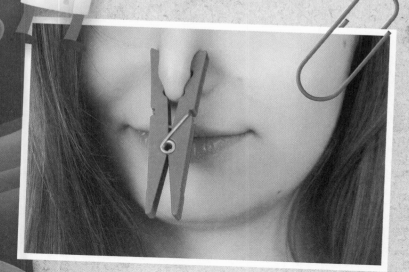

# Answers

### From pages 46-47

1. **D.** But some nerve signals might go even faster. Scientists learn new things about nerve signals all the time.

2. **C.** You don't realize you make so much, as most of it goes down your digestive tract with your food.

3. **C.** It's not the biggest, but the tongue packs the most power per square inch.

4. **D.** People say you can't do those things, but that's not true. You can tickle yourself (but only the roof of your mouth!); people with flexible joints really can lick their elbows; and you will still sneeze if you hold your eyelids open just as one erupts.

5. **D.** The Islets (pronounced EYE-lets) of Langerhans are clusters of pancreas cells that sense blood sugar levels and release insulin. They're named after the 22-year-old doctor who discovered them in 1869.

# The Human Body

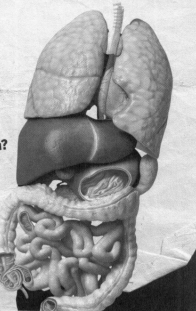

**11** **What is gross anatomy?**

A. Easy! It's all the things your body makes that are gross. Do I really need to list them?

B. The study of body parts and structures that can be seen with the eye

C. The study of the intestines

D. I don't know. And I don't want to know. Next question, please.

**12** **Your stomach does what every 3–4 days?**

A. Invites your pancreas over for some video gaming.

B. Balls into a giant knot because you forgot about homework that's due.

C. Produces a brand new lining.

D. Whips up a fresh batch of digestive acid.

**13** **Which is your weakest sense?**

A. The sense of smell. And that's a good thing, given my dog's breath.

B. The sense of taste. And that's a good thing, given the food at my school's cafeteria.

C. My sense of decency when my shorts tear in gym class.

D. My sixth sense. Because I don't even know what that's supposed to be.

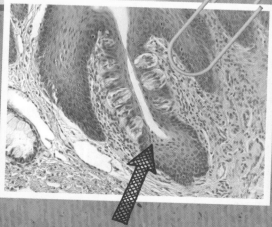

Taste buds

Answers on page 53

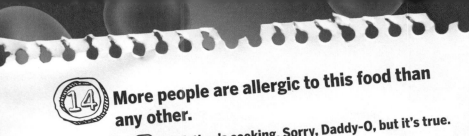

**(14) More people are allergic to this food than any other.**

- **A.** My father's cooking. Sorry, Daddy-O, but it's true.
- **B.** Wheat. I remember someone talking about going gluten-free.
- **C.** Dairy. Especially cow's milk.
- **D.** Fruitcake. There's a reason no one normal eats it.

**(15) Which of these is a real disorder in humans?**

- **A.** Maple Syrup Urine Disease
- **B.** Apple Belly Weight Gain Syndrome
- **C.** Chronic Garlic Sweat Disorder
- **D.** Genetic Elven Ear Protuberance

## Answers
### From pages 48-49

6. **A.** Pronounced BOR-boh-RIG-mee, it's the stomach rumble you get when you're hungry.

7. **B.** All the muscles that move your fingers are in your palm or forearm. They move your finger through tendons that are attached to the finger bones.

8. **A.** People lose so much skin (about 1.5 pounds a year) that the dust in homes is made largely of old skin bits. Gross!

9. **C.** Like your fingerprints, your tongue prints are unique to you.

10. **A.** You need airflow through your nose and sinuses to hum. Just try to hum a song with it pinched close!

# The Human Body

### 16  Why do you get goose bumps?

**A.** I stopped getting Goosebumps after Volume 14: *The Werewolf of Fever Swamp.* I've moved on to *The Hunger Games.*

**B.** To make you warmer or make you appear larger to enemies.

**C.** Ummm, is it because I'm afraid of geese? All that honking and squawking really freaks me out.

**D.** To make you able to swim farther and longer.

### 17  How long would it take for your tongue to freeze to an icy metal pole?

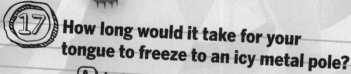

**A.** Instantly. I learned that the hard way.

**B.** Approximately 3 seconds. That's the time it takes for so-called friends to fall on the ground laughing.

**C.** Approximately 7 seconds. Which is about the time your brain will flash an image of your parents saying, "Are you really that stupid?"

**D.** Approximately 15 seconds. Which passes quickly when your pals are fumbling with their phones, trying to take a photo.

### 18  How many bacteria live on each square inch of your skin?

**A.** Hey! I shower every day. So none.

**B.** I count roughly nine. Or are those freckles?

**C.** Around 10,000

**D.** Around 32 million

Answers on page 55

**19** How long can you survive with nothing to eat?

**A.** Until suppertime. By then, I'm starving!

**B.** About 30-40 days

**C.** About a week

**D.** I'm not sure, but after about a day, my parents might not survive my complaining.

**20** When you're six years old, you do this about 300 times a day. By the time you're an adult, it drops to about 15 times a day.

**A.** Fart

**B.** Forget to change the cat litter

**C.** Blink

**D.** Laugh

# Answers
## From pages 50-51

11. **B.** If you enter a health-related profession, chances are you'll study gross anatomy at college.

12. **C.** If your stomach didn't produce a new lining regularly, it would digest itself along with your food!

13. **B.** Your sense of taste depends on your sense of smell and therefore has to play second fiddle to smell.

14. **C.** People who have allergic reactions to dairy products are called lactose intolerant. It's why many people can't have ice cream.

15. **A.** Maple Syrup Urine Disease is a blood-sugar disorder that makes your pee smell like maple syrup.

**21 How many teeth do humans have?**

A. Adults have 32. Kids have fewer.

B. It depends. For example, hockey players only have four.

C. Adults have 24. Kids have more.

D. 17, and I have proof: I bit into an apple and counted the marks. (Do I get extra credit for my genius, or what?)

**22 Which of these is healthiest to drink?**

A. Sports drinks. Full of sugar, salt, chemical flavoring, and artificial color— the four main food groups!

B. Water

C. Milk. A million ads can't be wrong!

D. A glass of all-purpose porpoise pus

Answers on page 57

**23** **Which of these is the most dangerous to your long-term health?**

**A.** Telling my brother he looks like a lumpy sock

**B.** Playing tuba. It never ends well for those guys.

**C.** Being a few pounds overweight

**D.** Getting a sunburn

**24** **To be safe, you need earplugs to do which of the following?**

**A.** Go to a football game.

**B.** Listen to someone talk about how good it was in the old days.

**C.** Sleep next to a dog dreaming of chasing squirrels.

**D.** Fly in an airplane.

## Answers
### From pages 52–53

**16.** **B.** Back when early humans were covered in fur, goose bumps made all that hair stand up if they were cold or threatened.

**17.** **A.** If the pole is cold enough, your tongue will freeze to it immediately. Don't do it!

**18.** **D** A recent scientific article noted that "human skin is crawling with bacteria." But don't worry—most of those bacteria are harmless to you.

**19.** **B.** It depends on each person, but usually you can survive about a month as long as you have water to drink.

**20.** **D.** Between episodes of *SpongeBob* and all those games of tag, kids laugh a lot more. See if you can keep it going into adulthood.

# The Human Body

**25** How many different smells can your nose pick out and remember?

A. My nose picks? Ahhhaaahhhaaaa!!!

B. About 50,000. Your nose is smart. Your nose knows.

C. About 2,000. After that, it all smells like old shoes.

D. About 250. Though it needn't bother, as all I want to smell is bacon or pizza.

**26** How many hairs are on a human head?

A. On average, about 100,000.

B. What about my uncle? He doesn't have any.

C. On average, about 10,000.

D. What about my gym teacher, Mr. Gorilla-with-a-whistle? He's got about 1,000,000, if you include his beard, nose, ears, eyebrows, and that weird mole on his cheek.

Answers on page 59

**27** **How many days can you go without sleep?**

**A.** I can't go even one day before I go face-first into my oatmeal.

**B.** Three days

**C.** Eleven days

**D.** Nine months. I'm not sure my history teacher has ever revealed consciousness to us.

**28** **Which of the following can cause dangerous reactions with many medicines?**

**A.** Grapefruit and grapefruit juice. Who knew?

**B.** A spoonful of sugar. Don't believe that silly song.

**C.** Hamster cage shavings. Which is good since they taste terrible.

**D.** Water. Crazy, huh?

## Answers

From pages 54-55

21. **A.** By the time they all come in during the teenage years, most adults have 32 teeth.

22. **B.** Water is, by far, the healthiest thing to drink. It's a myth that you need sports drinks when you exercise, unless you're running marathons.

23. **C.** Just one blistering sunburn before age 18 can double your chance of getting skin cancer later in life. Slap on that sunscreen!

24. **A.** One recent football game measured more than 137 decibels due to all the crowd noise in the stadium. Hearing damage can begin at only 85 decibels.

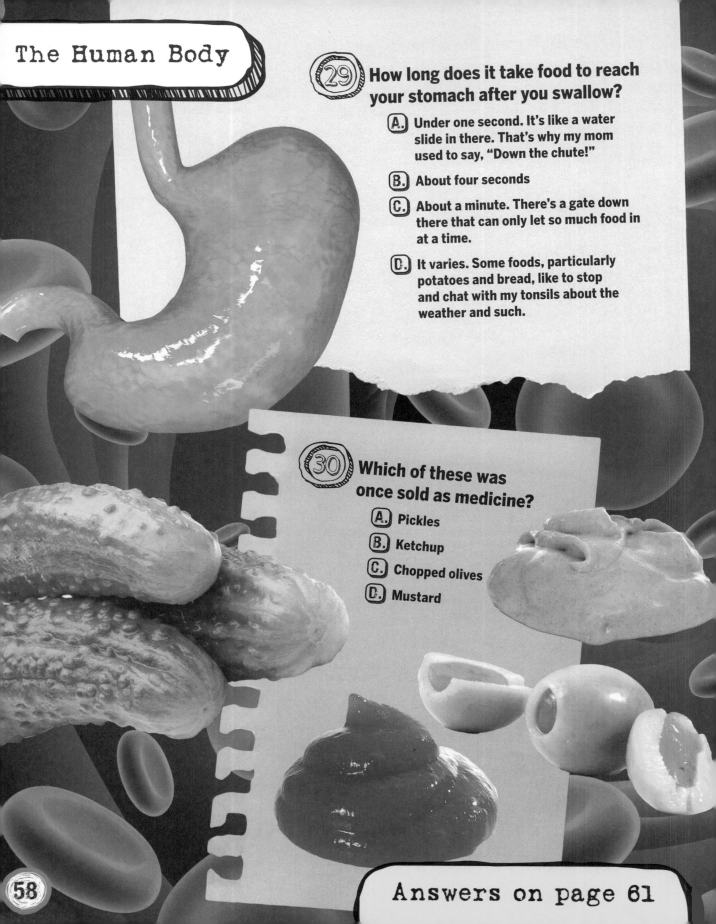

**29** How long does it take food to reach your stomach after you swallow?

A. Under one second. It's like a water slide in there. That's why my mom used to say, "Down the chute!"

B. About four seconds

C. About a minute. There's a gate down there that can only let so much food in at a time.

D. It varies. Some foods, particularly potatoes and bread, like to stop and chat with my tonsils about the weather and such.

**30** Which of these was once sold as medicine?

A. Pickles

B. Ketchup

C. Chopped olives

D. Mustard

Answers on page 61

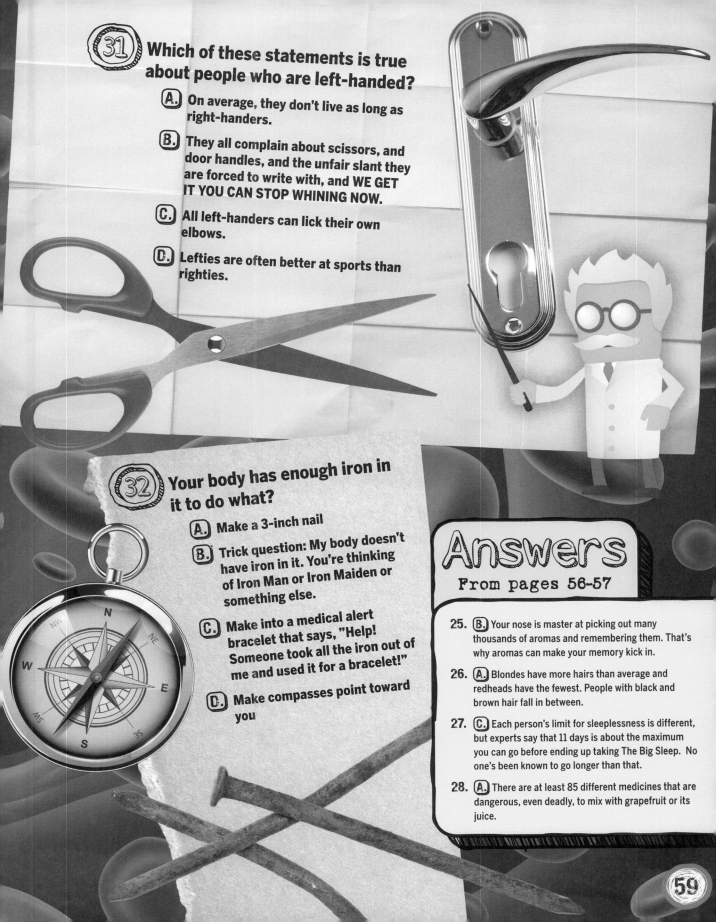

**31** **Which of these statements is true about people who are left-handed?**

A. On average, they don't live as long as right-handers.

B. They all complain about scissors, and door handles, and the unfair slant they are forced to write with, and WE GET IT YOU CAN STOP WHINING NOW.

C. All left-handers can lick their own elbows.

D. Lefties are often better at sports than righties.

**32** **Your body has enough iron in it to do what?**

A. Make a 3-inch nail

B. Trick question: My body doesn't have iron in it. You're thinking of Iron Man or Iron Maiden or something else.

C. Make into a medical alert bracelet that says, "Help! Someone took all the iron out of me and used it for a bracelet!"

D. Make compasses point toward you

## Answers
### From pages 56-57

25. **B.** Your nose is master at picking out many thousands of aromas and remembering them. That's why aromas can make your memory kick in.

26. **A.** Blondes have more hairs than average and redheads have the fewest. People with black and brown hair fall in between.

27. **C.** Each person's limit for sleeplessness is different, but experts say that 11 days is about the maximum you can go before ending up taking The Big Sleep. No one's been known to go longer than that.

28. **A.** There are at least 85 different medicines that are dangerous, even deadly, to mix with grapefruit or its juice.

# The Human Body

**33** Although your brain makes up only about 2.5 percent of your whole body, it uses 20 percent of what?

A. Scratching time?

B. The water you drink. It's where the expression "wet behind the ears" comes from.

C. The oxygen you breathe. It's where the expression "light-headed" comes from.

D. The calories you eat. It's where the expression "Are you dense?" comes from.

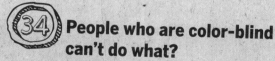

**34** People who are color-blind can't do what?

A. See color. I mean, duh! Do you want me to paint it red for you?

B. Dance. It's strange, but good color vision is directly linked to strong dancing ability.

C. Drive well. Yellow lines, white lines, red signs, green signs, it's all a blur.

D. See a certain range of colors.

Answers on page 63

**35** In 30 minutes, your body gives off enough heat to do which of these?

**A.** Boil a pot of water.

**B.** Make brothers, sisters, and pets complain you're too hot and sweaty to sit next to.

**C.** Cook an order of five scrambled eggs, two hash browns, four sausages, three strips of bacon, and one serving of wheat toast with melted butter.

**D.** Heat a horse barn for a week.

**36** If you could shrink yourself down enough to walk along every blood vessel in your body, how far would you have to walk?

**A.** About 60,000 miles. I better find something faster than walking!

**B.** About two miles. A calm 40-minute stroll, except I'd be a micrometer tall, inside a human body.

**C.** About 20 feet. Except in my foot. You can't have feet in a foot.

**D.** Zero. I figured it out: I'd grab a red blood cell and let the current take me everywhere.

# Answers
### From pages 58-59

29. **B.** A series of muscles move your food from your mouth to stomach, taking about four seconds with each swallow.

30. **B.** Many tomato concoctions were given fancy names and sold as medicine in the early 1800s. One such ketchup-based remedy was called "Dr. Miles' Compound Extract of Tomato."

31. **D.** Left-handers often make moves and shots right-handers aren't expecting, giving them an advantage in many sports.

32. **A.** Most of that iron is dissolved in your blood. Now if you could only pull a hammer out of your ear...

# True or False

1. The fingernail on your thumb grows the fastest.
   ⬜ T   ⬜ F

2. Your brain can feel pain.
   ⬜ T   ⬜ F

3. Sneezes leave your nose at up to 100 miles per hour.
   ⬜ T   ⬜ F

4. You have more bones when you're a baby.
   ⬜ T   ⬜ F

5. Your brain is more active during day than at night.
   ⬜ T   ⬜ F

6. It takes 17 muscles to smile but 43 to frown.
   ⬜ T   ⬜ F

Answers on page 148

**7** On a dark, clear night, a human eye can see 2,000-3,000 stars.

◯ T  ◯ F

**8** You pass gas, on average, 14 times per day.

◯ T  ◯ F

**9** Most people can't roll their tongue into a tube.

◯ T  ◯ F

**10** About one in 10 people are left-handed.

◯ T  ◯ F

**11** Snores can be almost as loud as a jackhammer.

◯ T  ◯ F

**12** Your eyes can see about 10,000 different colors!

◯ T  ◯ F

## Answers
### From pages 60-61

**33.** Ⓒ Your brain hogs way more oxygen than any other part of your body, but it needs it to help power that heavy-duty intellect of yours.

**34.** Ⓓ It's extremely rare not to be able to see any color at all. Most color blindness involves a small number of colors, such as certain blues or greens.

**35.** Ⓐ You could cook up some pasta! Bodies burn a heap of energy to maintain a constant body temperature that is usually much higher than the air temperature around them.

**36.** Ⓐ It would take you more than two years of walking nonstop to cover that distance.

# Space

## Can You Climb Out of *this* Black Hole?

**1** If you weigh exactly 100 pounds on Earth, how much would you weigh on the Moon?

**A.** 100 pounds. Why do you scientists always try to complicate things?

**B.** 100 pounds, 4 ounces. OK, you got me. I'd probably have eaten a few ounces of the cheese the Moon is made out of before getting on the scale.

**C.** 126.65 pounds. I'd have both Earth and Moon gravity affecting me.

**D.** 15.65 pounds. Which is about what I weighed when I was a year old.

**2** How long would your footprints stay on the Moon?

**A.** Forever! Or at least until a rival astronaut scuffs them out.

**B.** About 2.3 seconds. That assumes my parents are with me. Have you ever seen how fast the mop comes out when I track footprints into the house?

**C.** Six times less than on Earth, since the Moon is one-sixth the size.

**D.** A few days before the solar wind erases them.

Answers on page 67

**3** St. Paul, a city in the Canadian province of Alberta, is able to brag about which of these?

A. Winter temperatures as cold as interplanetary space.

B. Birthplace of Ziggy Stardust, the first musician to go to space.

C. The clearest views of the night sky on the entire planet.

D. First town on Earth to build a UFO landing pad.

**4** What happens if two metals touch in space?

A. They bounce off each other and float in opposite directions.

B. They fuse together.

C. They say "Excuse me!" and go about their business.

D. They get a warning under NASA's 'No Touching in Space' policy.

**5** How many times would Earth fit inside the Sun?

A. None. The Sun isn't some interstellar doghouse for any old mutt planet that needs a nap, you know.

B. Not even once. Can't you see how little the Sun is? If I hold a penny to my eye, I can block out the whole thing!

C. One million

D. 101. It's easy to remember because it's the same as the dalmatians.

**6** Four of the nine planets in our solar system have rings. Which has the most rings?

A. Probably Saturn

B. Probably Jupiter

C. Probably Ringtoss

D. What's with all the probablies? You should probably give a real answer, don't you think?

**7** What kind of planet is Pluto?

A. The same kind as Mickey, Minnie, Donald, and Daisy. Goofy, though, isn't a planet.

B. Dwarf planet

C. Asteroid planet

D. Ghost planet

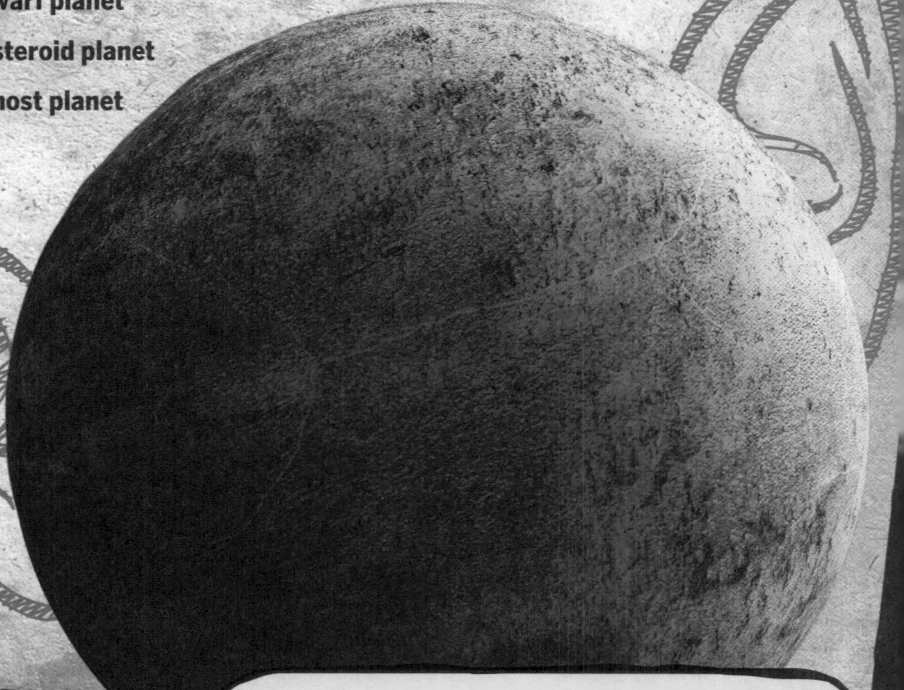

Answers on page 69

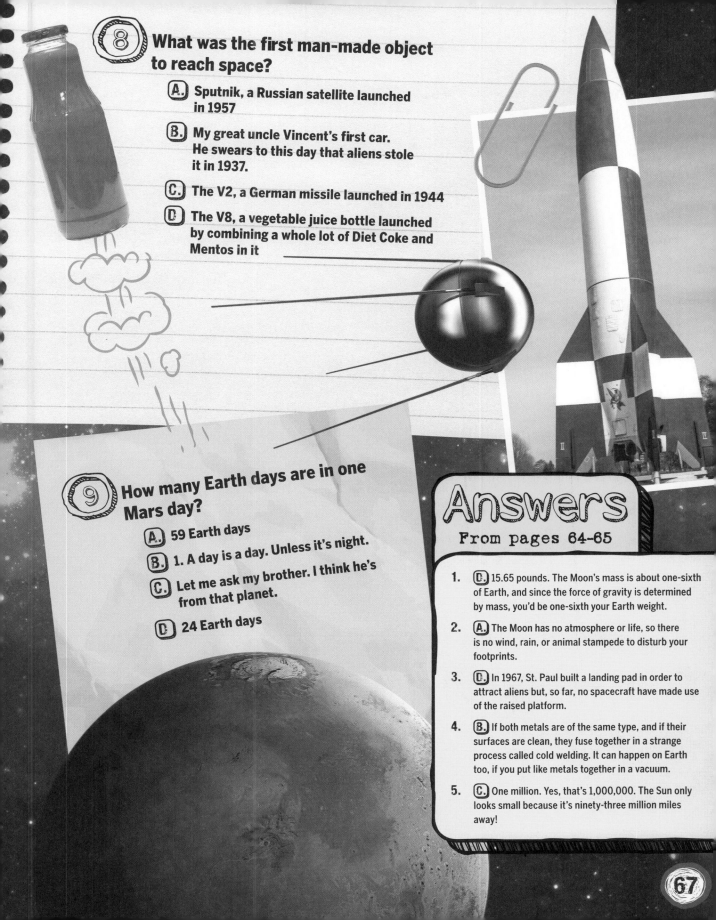

**8** What was the first man-made object to reach space?

**A.** Sputnik, a Russian satellite launched in 1957

**B.** My great uncle Vincent's first car. He swears to this day that aliens stole it in 1937.

**C.** The V2, a German missile launched in 1944

**D.** The V8, a vegetable juice bottle launched by combining a whole lot of Diet Coke and Mentos in it

**9** How many Earth days are in one Mars day?

**A.** 59 Earth days

**B.** 1. A day is a day. Unless it's night.

**C.** Let me ask my brother. I think he's from that planet.

**D.** 24 Earth days

## Answers
### From pages 64-65

1. **D.** 15.65 pounds. The Moon's mass is about one-sixth of Earth, and since the force of gravity is determined by mass, you'd be one-sixth your Earth weight.

2. **A.** The Moon has no atmosphere or life, so there is no wind, rain, or animal stampede to disturb your footprints.

3. **D.** In 1967, St. Paul built a landing pad in order to attract aliens but, so far, no spacecraft have made use of the raised platform.

4. **B.** If both metals are of the same type, and if their surfaces are clean, they fuse together in a strange process called cold welding. It can happen on Earth too, if you put like metals together in a vacuum.

5. **C.** One million. Yes, that's 1,000,000. The Sun only looks small because it's ninety-three million miles away!

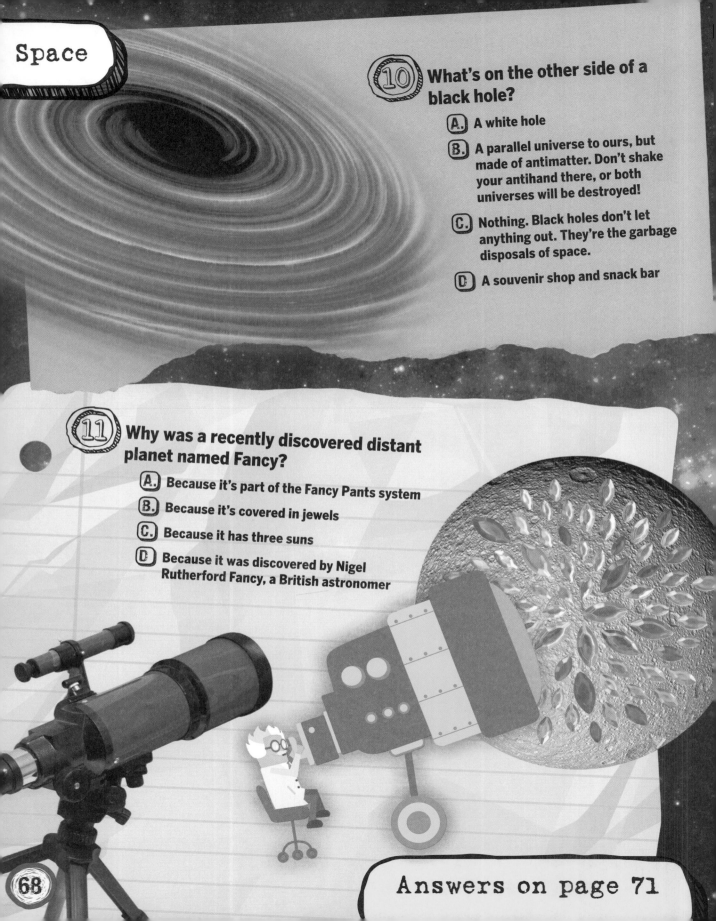

**10** What's on the other side of a black hole?

A. A white hole

B. A parallel universe to ours, but made of antimatter. Don't shake your antihand there, or both universes will be destroyed!

C. Nothing. Black holes don't let anything out. They're the garbage disposals of space.

D. A souvenir shop and snack bar

**11** Why was a recently discovered distant planet named Fancy?

A. Because it's part of the Fancy Pants system

B. Because it's covered in jewels

C. Because it has three suns

D. Because it was discovered by Nigel Rutherford Fancy, a British astronomer

Answers on page 71

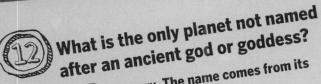

**12** **What is the only planet not named after an ancient god or goddess?**

**A.** Mercury. The name comes from its silvery surface.

**B.** Uranus. It's named after, well, let's just say the conference room of young male scientists couldn't stop giggling when they came up with the name.

**C.** Pluto. It's named after Mickey's dog.

**D.** You're standing on it.

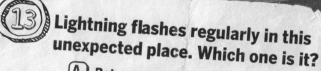

**13** **Lightning flashes regularly in this unexpected place. Which one is it?**

**A.** Between my uncles when there's only one hamburger left on the platter

**B.** Around any spaceship not covered with anti-lightning material

**C.** Within meteor showers

**D.** In the middle of space

## Answers
### From pages 66-67

6. **A.** Probably Saturn. Planetary rings are hard to count because they're jumbled together. Saturn has 7-30 rings. The other planets with rings: Jupiter, Neptune, and Uranus.

7. **B.** Discovered in 1930, Pluto was first considered to be a regular planet. In 2006, it was reclassified as a dwarf planet, which technically means it is no longer a planet at all.

8. **C.** In World War II, Germany created a missile called the V2. It traveled beyond Earth's atmosphere during a test flight.

9. **A.** Mars rotates so slowly that 59 days pass here on Earth before the red planet completes one turn.

**14** How many stars are in our galaxy?

**A.** 100-400 billion. Give or take a few billion.

**B.** There's only one true star in the galaxy. (We love you, Miley!)

**C.** 807,432,879. Interestingly, the person who counted them got paid a penny per star, and so retired a millionaire.

**D.** It depends on whether it's a clear or cloudy night.

**15** What is the name of our galaxy?

**A.** The Mars Bar

**B.** The Milky Way

**C.** The Samsung Galaxy

**D.** Fred

**16** What is the main ingredient in our Sun?

**A.** Hydrogen. It's like a giant bomb.

**B.** Helium, which is why it has a squeaky voice.

**C.** Trillions of socks, all missing from the laundry.

**D.** Sunshine, of course. Just like my dear grandma.

Answers on page 73

**17** **What is this photo of?**

A. Spirit, a Mars rover

B. The Internet

C. The International Space Station

D. Yoda's winter vacation home

**18** In 1971, an astronaut took 400 seeds to the Moon before planting them back on Earth. What grew from them?

A. Trees. Moon trees.

B. Sunflowers

C. Pet rocks

D. Watermelons the size of a small car

# Answers
## From pages 68-69

10. **A.** After a black hole sucks everything in, scientists increasingly believe it shoots stuff out through a white hole somewhere else in the universe. Really. Look it up.

11. **B.** Discovered in 2012, Fancy is trillions of miles from Earth and has a surface made of graphite and diamonds!

12. **D.** Earth. All other planet names in our solar system are named for Greek and Roman gods.

13. **D.** The power in each lightning bolt in space can be the equivalent of a trillion bolts here on Earth!

**19** What is the only planet in our system that rotates clockwise?

A. Saturn. It's those crazy rings. They got things spinning out of control.

B. Earth. After all, we invented the word "clockwise."

C. Mars. Most things on Mars are backwards.

D. Venus. That's just how it rolls.

**20** What is the Vomit Comet?

A. What I call my little sister

B. A popular nickname for the Space Mountain roller coaster at Walt Disney World

C. Regurgatarius—a fast-moving comet in the outer part of the solar system

D. An airplane used to simulate zero gravity

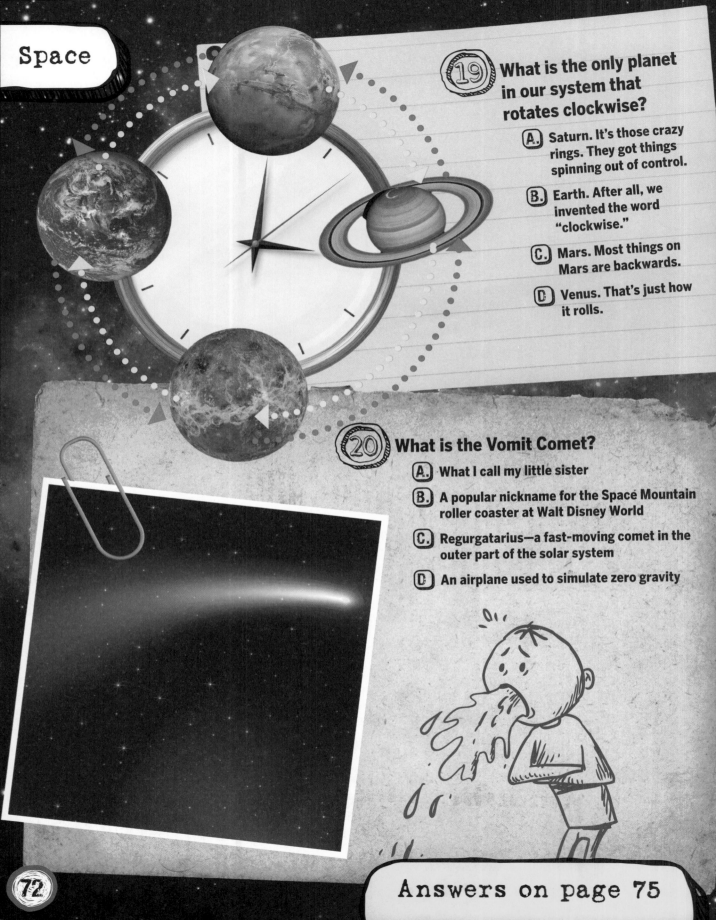

Answers on page 75

## 21 How many man-made objects are in orbit around Earth?

**A.** More than ten million. Next, several space ships need to take garbage bags with them and clean up a little.

**B.** Roughly 800,000. More than 50 years of regular space travel and satellite launches have left a lot of debris.

**C.** 4,233. Mostly it's old satellites, rocket ship boosters, and my dad's lost golf balls.

**D.** One. The Moon. Didn't we cover this already?

## 22 In addition to talking with members of their flight team, astronauts use their helmet microphones to do which of these?

**A.** Beatbox

**B.** Scratch their nose

**C.** Call their mom

**D.** Imitate the voice of Darth Vader

## Answers
### From pages 70-71

14. **A.** Scientists estimate there are somewhere between 100-400 billion stars in our galaxy.

15. **B.** Our galaxy is called the Milky Way because the light from its billions of stars looks like thin milk from our earthly viewpoint.

16. **A.** The Sun is about 71 percent hydrogen, a highly explosive gas.

17. **C.** The International Space Station. Since 2000, astronauts from more than 15 countries have spent time living and working on the ISS.

18. **A.** Stuart Roosa, an Apollo 14 astronaut, brought the tree seeds back and gave them to many people. Most of the trees are in unknown locations, but the ones we do know about are still growing strong!

**23** Which heavenly object is shown here?

A. The Big Dipper

B. The Little Dipper

C. The Skinny Dipper

D. The Zip-a-Dee-Doo-Dah

**24** What is the Big Dipper useful for?

A. It helps you tell the time; when it's directly above you, it's midnight.

B. It makes parents feel smart, as it's the one constellation they can point out to their children.

C. It points to north. Very handy when you're lost in a dark forest.

D. It holds most of the universe's fresh water.

**25** How many moons does Earth have?

A. 12. One for each month.

B. One. Definitely.

C. Two. Maybe.

D. It's obvious your spacesuit is leaking oxygen or something. Get medical help.

Answers on page 77

**26** Jupiter has a very famous feature on its face. What is it called?

A. The Great Red Spot. Because even a planet like Jupiter deserves a pet dog.

B. The Great Red Zit. Get that planet some acne cream!

C. The Great Red Jacobisawesome. Because they asked the intern to name it.

D. The Great Red Nose. Because it's really cold that far out in space.

**27** Because of this, birds can never survive in outer space:

A. Because it's space. No oxygen? Freezing cold? Helloooo??

B. They can't swallow. Not even the swallows. Get it? Ha!

C. They can't help but peck through their helmets like eggshells.

D. There's nothing for their wings to push against.

# Answers
## From pages 72-73

19. **C.** No one understands why Venus rotates in the opposite direction to all other planets.

20. **C.** Also called a "reduced gravity aircraft." It flies in a way that gives astronauts the illusion of weightlessness and usually makes them vomit at first.

21. **A.** There are more than ten million objects orbiting Earth. Some are big, like satellites and telescopes; a lot of them are just pieces of space junk.

22. **B.** They can't reach their nose with their hands so, if it itches, they rub it on their microphone.

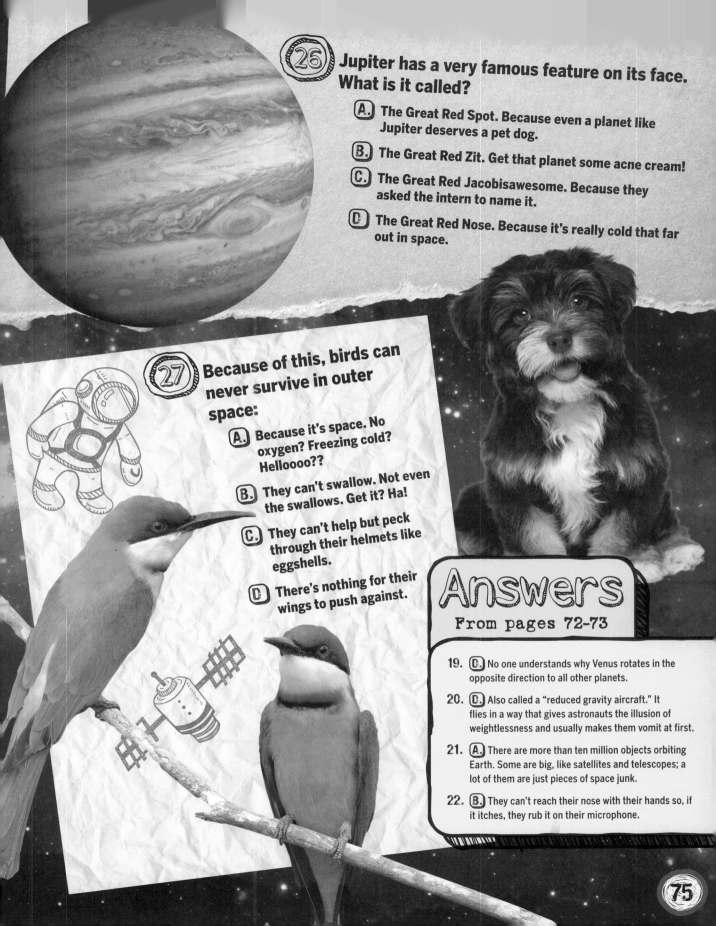

**28** Which of these can you do on the surface of Venus?

A. Bake a pizza. With no oven. In about a minute.

B. Kick a soccer ball five miles.

C. Go on the rides at Six Flags Over Venus.

D. Get really good views of the stars at night.

**29** We on Earth always see the same side of the Moon. We never get to see the back, or "dark" side. Why is that?

A. It's a little insecure about how that side looks, so it always reveals its good side.

B. Strangely, that's how Earth commands it.

C. Because it doesn't rotate. It just floats motionless over us.

D. Maybe it only has one side. Did you ever think of that?

**30** What is a "gas giant?"

A. It's a kid in my class. He's really tall. He always has gas.

B. It's a type of star.

C. They also call them solar flares, but we know what the Sun is really doing.

D. It's a type of planet.

Answers on page 79

**31** Which of these companies beamed an advertisement into space for aliens?

**A.** Doritos. Even Martians need snacks when watching sports on television.

**B.** Coca-Cola. But it was a flop because aliens exploded from the gas.

**C.** NASA. New recruits have to come from somewhere.

**D.** Wal-Mart. Insert your own joke here.

**32** What is this?

**A.** The eye of Sauron

**B.** A black hole

**C.** A nebula

**D.** My TV screen after it was hit with a Wii controller

# Answers
### From pages 74–75

**23.** **A.** Found in the skies of the Northern Hemisphere, the Big Dipper is a group of stars that looks like a drinking ladle.

**24.** **C.** Trace a line through the two stars on the right and extend it upward. The next star along that line is the North Star.

**25.** **C.** In 1999, astronomers discovered a three-mile-wide asteroid that appears to be caught in Earth's gravitational grip—if confirmed, that would make it another moon. Its name is Cruithne and it takes 770 years to complete a U-shaped orbit around Earth.

**26.** **A.** The Great Red Spot, also called Jupiter's Eye, is a huge storm that has been raging for at least 400 years.

**27.** **B.** Birds can't swallow without gravity and would starve in space. Humans have muscles in their throats that propel food down, with or without gravity.

# Space

**33** What causes a Moon crater?

A. Space rocks crashing into the surface

B. Incredibly intense space storms

C. Too many spacecraft landings

D. The cow doesn't always jump over the Moon. It smacked into it a lot, too.

**34** What would happen if you spit into space?

A. It would freeze instantly.

B. It would become an Everlasting Gobstopper and orbit the earth.

C. Yuck! That's disgusting!

D. It would boil instantly.

**35** What is the scientific phrase used to describe the beginning of the universe?

A. The Bourne Paradox

B. The Big Bang

C. The universe has always existed. It has no beginning or end.

D. Let me ask my dad. He's old enough to remember.

Answers on page 81

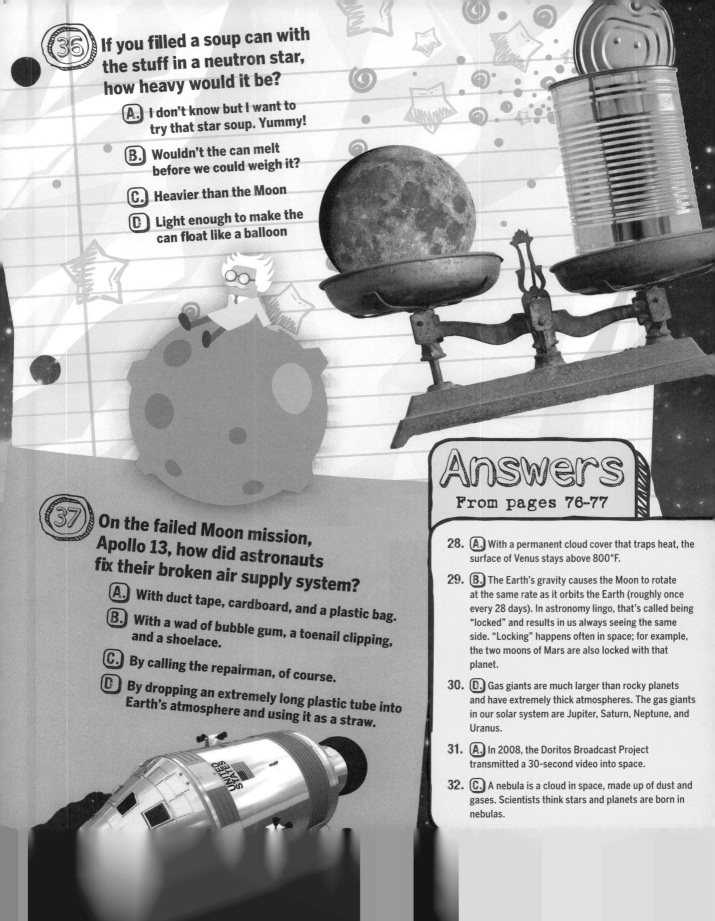

**36** If you filled a soup can with the stuff in a neutron star, how heavy would it be?

A. I don't know but I want to try that star soup. Yummy!

B. Wouldn't the can melt before we could weigh it?

C. Heavier than the Moon

D. Light enough to make the can float like a balloon

**37** On the failed Moon mission, Apollo 13, how did astronauts fix their broken air supply system?

A. With duct tape, cardboard, and a plastic bag.

B. With a wad of bubble gum, a toenail clipping, and a shoelace.

C. By calling the repairman, of course.

D. By dropping an extremely long plastic tube into Earth's atmosphere and using it as a straw.

## Answers
### From pages 76–77

28. **A.** With a permanent cloud cover that traps heat, the surface of Venus stays above 800°F.

29. **B.** The Earth's gravity causes the Moon to rotate at the same rate as it orbits the Earth (roughly once every 28 days). In astronomy lingo, that's called being "locked" and results in us always seeing the same side. "Locking" happens often in space; for example, the two moons of Mars are also locked with that planet.

30. **C.** Gas giants are much larger than rocky planets and have extremely thick atmospheres. The gas giants in our solar system are Jupiter, Saturn, Neptune, and Uranus.

31. **A.** In 2008, the Doritos Broadcast Project transmitted a 30-second video into space.

32. **C.** A nebula is a cloud in space, made up of dust and gases. Scientists think stars and planets are born in nebulas.

# True or False

1. Pluto is bigger than our Moon.
   - ☐ T   ☐ F

2. Jupiter is the largest planet in our solar system.
   - ☐ T   ☐ F

3. It takes 27.32 days for the Moon to orbit Earth.
   - ☐ T   ☐ F

4. Thirty people have been to the surface of the Moon, including one guy who took a very wrong turn on the way to the grocery store.
   - ☐ T   ☐ F

5. The Sun's core is twenty-seven million degrees Fahrenheit.
   - ☐ T   ☐ F

6. Currently there are two operating space stations in Earth's orbit.
   - ☐ T   ☐ F

7. A NASA spacesuit weighs about 280 lbs.
   - ☐ T   ☐ F

Answers on pages 148-149

**8** The Sun burns with a yellow color.

◻ T      ◻ F

**9** Mars has four moons.

◻ T      ◻ F

**10** It takes light more than eight minutes to reach Earth from the Sun.

◻ T      ◻ F

**11** Outer space is empty.

◻ T      ◻ F

**12** The first food astronauts ate in space was a salami sandwich.

◻ T      ◻ F

**13** In 2013, China landed a Moon rover. Its name was Jade Rabbit.

◻ T      ◻ F

**14** All stars are the same size.

◻ T      ◻ F

**15** Planets orbit the Sun in circles.

◻ T      ◻ F

# Answers

## From pages 78-79

33. **A.** Meteors and asteroids crashing into the Moon have given it a pockmarked surface.

34. **D.** The boiling point of water (or spit) depends on pressure, not temperature. With zero pressure in space, it boils instantly!

35. **B.** The most accepted scientific theory for the beginning of the universe is the Big Bang: a massive explosion that threw matter across the universe.

36. **C.** Neutron stars are extremely dense and made of matter much heavier than anything on our planet.

37. **A.** It was an ugly repair, but it allowed Apollo 13 to limp home safely.

# ACK EXAM 5

## Art

### You'll Know It when You See It

**1) What is art?**

**A.** Art is the funny-looking guy who cleans my school.

**B.** It's stuff that serves no purpose other than to be looked at (for example, purple hair).

**C.** It's painting stuff, except not the kind where you paint your bedroom (or your dog—hey, it was a mistake!).

**D.** It's when you create or perform something to express your inner feelings or emotions.

**2) How does doodling help you become an artist?**

**A.** When your teachers see you doing it, they give you detention, where you have lots of time to practice arty stuff.

**B.** Well, it doesn't help you exactly, but if you make really great doodles in your textbooks, it can inspire the next kids who get them.

**C.** It increases creativity and focus.

**D.** Constant doodling leads to really bad grades, leaving you no career choice but to doodle for a living.

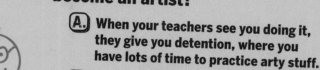

Answers on page 85

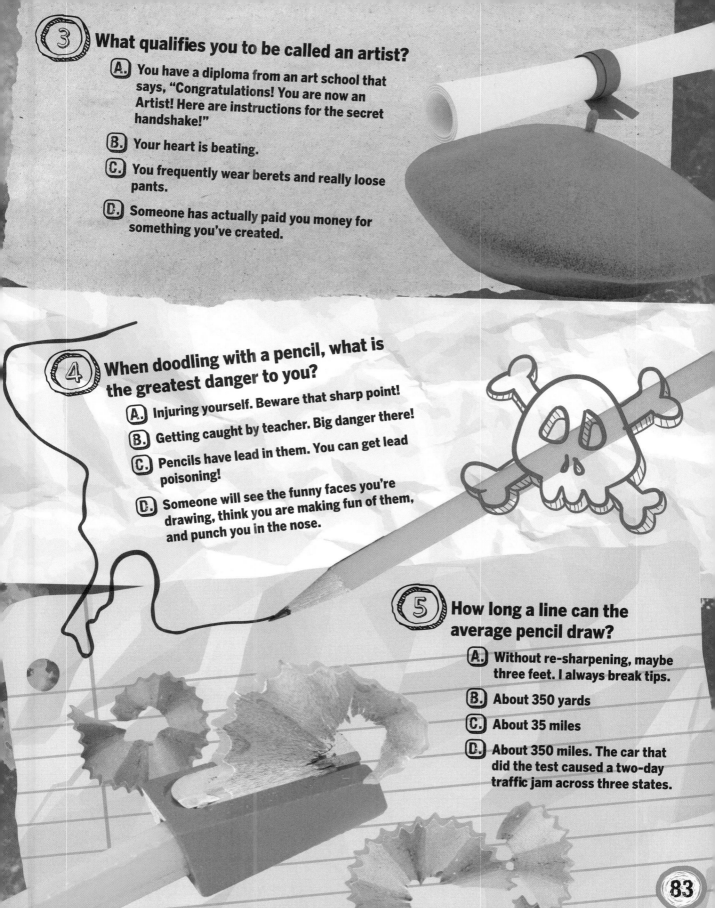

### ③ What qualifies you to be called an artist?

**A.** You have a diploma from an art school that says, "Congratulations! You are now an Artist! Here are instructions for the secret handshake!"

**B.** Your heart is beating.

**C.** You frequently wear berets and really loose pants.

**D.** Someone has actually paid you money for something you've created.

### ④ When doodling with a pencil, what is the greatest danger to you?

**A.** Injuring yourself. Beware that sharp point!

**B.** Getting caught by teacher. Big danger there!

**C.** Pencils have lead in them. You can get lead poisoning!

**D.** Someone will see the funny faces you're drawing, think you are making fun of them, and punch you in the nose.

### ⑤ How long a line can the average pencil draw?

**A.** Without re-sharpening, maybe three feet. I always break tips.

**B.** About 350 yards

**C.** About 35 miles

**D.** About 350 miles. The car that did the test caused a two-day traffic jam across three states.

**6** This is one of the world's most famous paintings. What was the name of the Dutch artist who painted it?

A. Vincent van Gogh

B. Rembrandt Harmenszoon van Rijn

C. Rip van Winkle. It took him 20 years to paint.

D. Hollandaise van Sauce

**7** How many paintings did Vincent van Gogh sell during his lifetime of making great art?

A. All of them. How else could he afford to build that big museum of his work in Amsterdam?

B. One. Out of more than 900. It takes a while for genius to be recognized.

C. 35. And they were all self-portraits. Odd, as he wasn't a very handsome guy.

D. None. In his day, he bartered. For *Starry Night* he got five chickens and a bushel of apples.

Answers on page 87

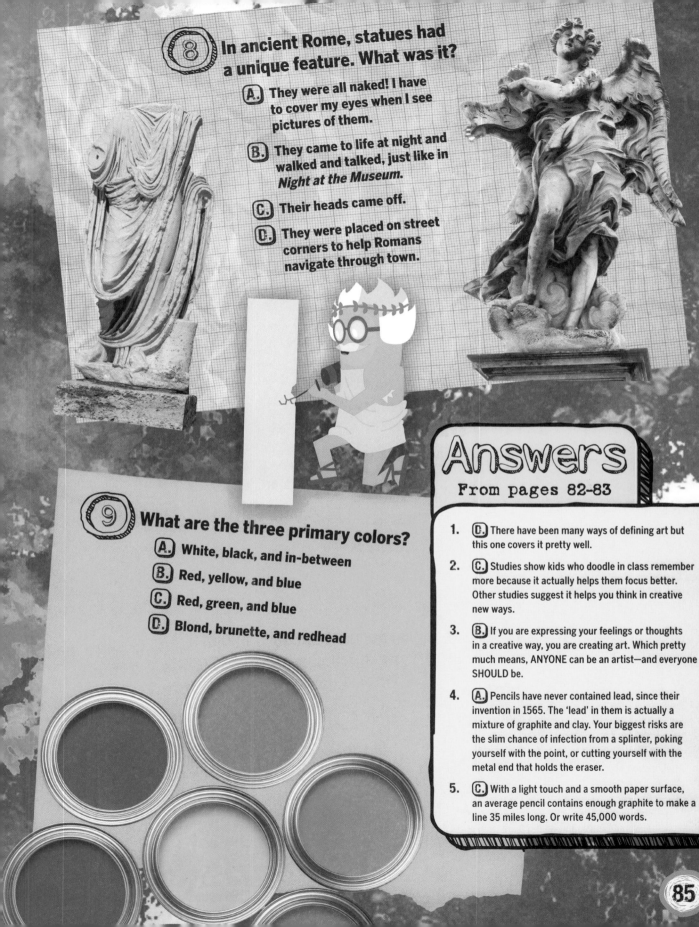

**8** In ancient Rome, statues had a unique feature. What was it?

**A.** They were all naked! I have to cover my eyes when I see pictures of them.

**B.** They came to life at night and walked and talked, just like in *Night at the Museum*.

**C.** Their heads came off.

**D.** They were placed on street corners to help Romans navigate through town.

**9** What are the three primary colors?

**A.** White, black, and in-between

**B.** Red, yellow, and blue

**C.** Red, green, and blue

**D.** Blond, brunette, and redhead

# Answers
## From pages 82-83

1. **D.** There have been many ways of defining art but this one covers it pretty well.

2. **C.** Studies show kids who doodle in class remember more because it actually helps them focus better. Other studies suggest it helps you think in creative new ways.

3. **B.** If you are expressing your feelings or thoughts in a creative way, you are creating art. Which pretty much means, ANYONE can be an artist—and everyone SHOULD be.

4. **A.** Pencils have never contained lead, since their invention in 1565. The 'lead' in them is actually a mixture of graphite and clay. Your biggest risks are the slim chance of infection from a splinter, poking yourself with the point, or cutting yourself with the metal end that holds the eraser.

5. **C.** With a light touch and a smooth paper surface, an average pencil contains enough graphite to make a line 35 miles long. Or write 45,000 words.

**10** People have been painting for at least 20,000 years. But how long did they have to wait to be able to buy ready-mixed color paints?

**A.** Not until the paint company Sherwin-Williams started offering the product in 1880.

**B.** Not until Thomas Edison invented that crazy can-shaking machine in 1904.

**C.** Not until a red apple and green pear dropped on Sir Isaac Newton's head at the same time in 1703.

**D.** Not until Nero, the emperor of Rome, declared that all Roman citizens had to paint the town red in the year 58 A.D.

**11** What is a painting of a bowl of fruit an example of?

**A.** Artistic torture. I want to eat it, but I can't.

**B.** A still life

**C.** Hotel art

**D.** A totally yummy smoothie recipe

**12** The most famous still life paintings were made by Dutch painters in the 1500s and 1600s. What is noteworthy about them?

**A.** The artists would sneak a self-portrait onto a piece of fruit. Look carefully at the grapes!

**B.** They were actually painted to be advertisements for food shops. Artists have to make a living, you know.

**C.** Look carefully, and you'll see a whole lot of bugs. Yuck!

**D.** By Dutch law, every painting needed to include at least one tulip.

Answers on page 89

**13** What do experts say is the most fascinating thing to look at in paintings with people in them?

A. The price tag. Some of those things go for millions.

B. The clothes they're wearing. Or not wearing, as the case may be.

C. The eyes

D. The feet

**14** This is often considered the most famous American painting. What is it called?

A. *The Simpsons*

B. *American Gothic*

C. *The Simple Life*

D. *When that No-Good Son of Mine Gets Home I'm Going to...*

# Answers

### From pages 84-85

6. **A.** Born in 1853, van Gogh is one of the most popular painters of all time, thanks to the bold colors, beauty, and emotion of his art. This painting, *Starry Night*, is a great example.

7. **B.** Van Gogh only sold one painting while he was alive. It's called *The Red Vineyard at Arles*. He lived his entire life in poverty, and suffered from mental illness.

8. **C.** Statues of dignitaries were made with detachable heads, so that if one official fell out of favor, his head could be removed and replaced by another.

9. **B.** Primary colors exist all by themselves. All other colors are made by blending primary colors together (along with white and black to vary the lightness).

**15** What was the special ingredient in the paint pigment known as Mummy Brown?

A. Mummies

B. Brownies

C. Chunks of the Great Pyramids ground into dust

D. Gravy from a popular recipe called "Mum's Best Meatloaf"

**16** What is the origin of the word "graffiti?"

A. It's Italian for "scratched."

B. Roman street artists yelled it when they spotted police coming. It translates to, "Look out, fellow street artists! Police are coming!"

C. It comes from graphite, the same stuff in pencils. It was the first thing used to mark graffiti.

D. It meant, "Yo! Let's go tag that wall!" in ancient Greek.

Answers on page 91

## 17. What makes mosaic art different?

A. It can only be displayed with music playing.

B. It doesn't require any paint or dye.

C. It can only be made by someone with the first or last name of Moses.

D. It's the only art made to be walked on.

## 18. This work is by a graphic artist named M.C. Escher. What is the name for this type of artwork?

A. Crazy. Nutso. Cuckoo. Wacko. Any of these will do.

B. The coolest thing ever. Look at those little guys going up and up and up!

C. Infinite loops

D. Impossible constructions

# Answers

## From pages 86-87

**10.** **A.** In 1880, the paint company Sherwin-Williams found a way to keep colors suspended in an oil base. Until then, everyone had to mix their own colors and use them up quickly before they separated.

**11.** **B.** A still life is a painting of everyday objects, often bowls of fruit or vases of flowers. Unusual colors and perspectives make it seem like you're seeing something familiar in an entirely new way.

**12.** **C.** In their pursuit of perfect realism, the classic Dutch still life paintings often include many flying and crawling insects. And, sometimes, the fruit or flowers are drooping or turning rotten!

**13.** **C.** We humans naturally look first at each other's eyes. In a portrait, you can get a strong sense of the character from his or her eyes. Plus, it's fascinating to see the brush strokes and delicate techniques artists use to paint eyes.

**14.** **B.** Artist Grant Wood used his sister and his dentist as models for *American Gothic*, his 1930 painting set in front of a rural house in Eldon, Iowa. Gothic refers to the architectural style of house, which is called Carpenter Gothic.

**19** This painting is call *Le Bateau* (*The Boat*), and is by the beloved modern artist Henri Matisse. What is noteworthy about it?

A. It's the only work by Matisse that no one was willing to buy.

B. It was hung upside down at the Museum of Modern Art in New York, and no one noticed for 47 days.

C. Matisse, when he completed it, called it *Le Piece of Junk*. Then he sold it for $1.2 million.

D. It was actually made by Matisse's four-year-old nephew.

**20** Which of these did the most for turning everyday people into instant artists?

A. A law that passed in 1930, requiring all children to be able to paint portraits of their mothers

B. The invention of water-based paint, also called watercolors

C. The rise of psychiatrists. Ever since, parents have been told to tell their children how wonderful their drawings are, and to call them "budding artists."

D. The paint-by-number kit

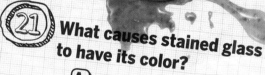

**21** What causes stained glass to have its color?

A. Stains, of course. A splash of tomato sauce, and that red is there forever. (Sorry, Mom, I KNOW it was your favorite tablecloth.)

B. Chemical elements. Like periodic-table-of-elements stuff.

C. They're like mood rings. Their color changes if they're happy, sappy, sad, mad, gassy, sassy, lovey, or dovey.

D. Mummy Brown pigment

Answers on page 93

**22** What size is the world's biggest paint-by-numbers work?

**A.** The one in my grandpa's den, of dogs playing cards. Grandma says it's the world's biggest eyesore.

**B.** Just over 40,000 square feet. But who has square feet, and how do they paint with them?

**C.** The size of a soccer field, nearly 78,000 square feet.

**D.** The Painted Desert in Arizona, at 3.9 billion square feet.

**23** What is the term used to describe the painting style where you can't really tell what the subject of the painting is?

**A.** Graffiti

**B.** Abstract

**C.** Impressionism

**D.** Ugly

# Answers
## From pages 88-89

15. **A.** Mummy Brown pigment added a deep burnt-looking color to paints in the 1500s and 1600s. It got its color from powder made of ground-up mummies from Egypt, both human and cat.

16. **A.** "Graffiato" is the Italian word for scratched. Early graffiti didn't use spray paint. It was made simply by scratching designs into surfaces.

17. **B.** Mosaic art is made by arranging pieces of stone, tiles, or glass to make a picture or pattern. No painting is involved, but you do need a lot of adhesive!

18. **D.** Escher, who died in 1972, was most famous for his pioneering artwork called impossible constructions. These works looked plausible as a painting, but are impossible to exist in real life.

**24** The sculpture *David*, made by Michelangelo based on the Bible hero, is widely considered one of the best sculptures ever created. Which of the following is true?

**A.** Michelangelo was the third artist chosen to make the sculpture from the same piece of marble.

**B.** It was supposed to be covered by a cloth toga, but the wind kept blowing it off, and no one complained, so they let him remain naked.

**C.** When the Pope first saw it, he said, "Magnificent! But he needs a toga."

**D.** Michelangelo nearly finished a companion sculpture called Goliath, but it fell over and shattered.

**25** What is a focal point?

**A.** When talking about art, the place or item that catches your eye first

**B.** The place where artists gather for coffee and discussion

**C.** The point at the top of a crayon

**D.** It's when the eyes in a painting seem to follow you everywhere. Creepy!

Focal Point Frappucino

Answers on page 95

**26** So what IS it called when the eyes of someone in a painting seem to follow you?

- **A.** Ubiquitous gaze
- **B.** Gazeo creepio
- **C.** Gazeous maximus
- **D.** Amazing gaze

 **27** The painter who made this image is named Andy Warhol. What school of art did he make popular?

- **A.** Advertising
- **B.** The Play With Your Food Society
- **C.** Pop Art
- **D.** The Mmmmm Mmmmm Good Movement

## Answers

### From pages 90-91

19. **B.** The mistake was discovered in 1961 by a stockbroker, who notified the New York Times, which then notified the museum.

20. **D.** In 1951, the Palmer Paint Company in Detroit, Michigan, began selling paint-by-number kits with two brushes, dozens of premixed colors of paint, and a canvas with numbered spaces. Millions of kids and adults snapped them up.

21. **B.** Elements such as cobalt, gold, uranium, lead, and copper are added to glass as it's made and are forever cemented in its structure. So the color never fades even though sunlight hits windows made from stained glass for many centuries.

22. **B.** It took more than 1,500 people to make the 40,000-square-foot painting in Pakistan in 2013. That's nearly one acre!

23. **B.** Abstract art doesn't try to represent recognizable reality. Rather, it uses colors, shapes, and texture to create mood and emotion.

**28** How does an Etch-A-Sketch erase itself?

**A.** The secret is... leprechauns and gremlins!

**B.** The secret is...magnets and iron dust!

**C.** The secret is...salami and mustard!

**D.** The secret is...aluminum and little balls!

**29** When did cartoons begin?

**A.** 20,000 years ago. Archeologists recently discovered cave paintings of mastodons with silly mustaches and googly eyeballs.

**B.** 600 years ago. The word emerged in the Middle Ages to mean any preparatory drawing for a piece of art.

**C.** 200 years ago. With the rise of newspapers came the rise of drawing politicians to look like bumbling fools.

**D.** 1928, when Mickey Mouse first appeared in an animated feature.

Answers on page 97

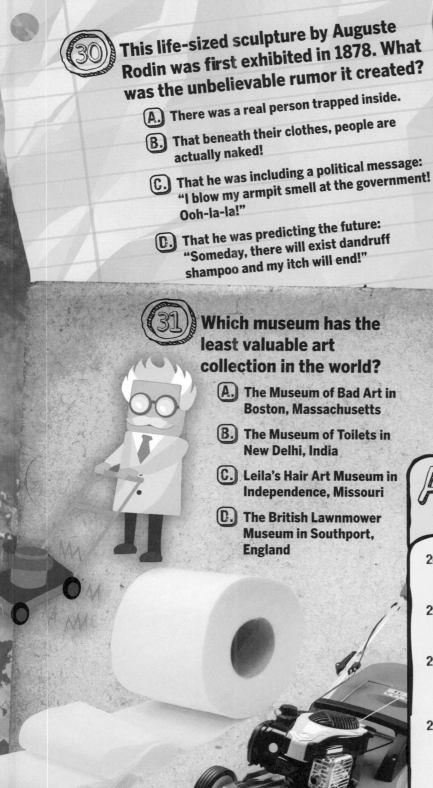

**30** This life-sized sculpture by Auguste Rodin was first exhibited in 1878. What was the unbelievable rumor it created?

- **A.** There was a real person trapped inside.
- **B.** That beneath their clothes, people are actually naked!
- **C.** That he was including a political message: "I blow my armpit smell at the government! Ooh-la-la!"
- **D.** That he was predicting the future: "Someday, there will exist dandruff shampoo and my itch will end!"

**31** Which museum has the least valuable art collection in the world?

- **A.** The Museum of Bad Art in Boston, Massachusetts
- **B.** The Museum of Toilets in New Delhi, India
- **C.** Leila's Hair Art Museum in Independence, Missouri
- **D.** The British Lawnmower Museum in Southport, England

## Answers
From pages 92-93

24. **A.** The piece of marble sat outdoors for 10 years between the first two artists' work, and 25 years more prior to Michelangelo taking over the work.

25. **A.** The focal point is also called the center of interest. It is the place on a work of art that your eye is naturally drawn toward.

26. **A.** Ubiquitous means everywhere, so it's a gaze that goes everywhere. The artistic effect is also called pursuing eyes, which may be even creepier than the phenomenon itself.

27. **C.** Pop Art is a school of art that began in the 1950s and uses product labels, images of movie stars, advertisements, and other commonplace items with the aim of making art more fun and more recognizable to lots of people. Andy Warhol is the best known of the Pop Artists.

95

# Art

 **32** **Why do so many artists paint self-portraits?**

**A.** Because they're really, really vain. How else could you be an artist?

**B.** Because they can't afford plastic surgery, and fix their faces through their art.

**C.** Because models are expensive, hard to find, and don't like sitting perfectly still for days on end.

**D.** Because they use the images for their holiday newsletters to family.

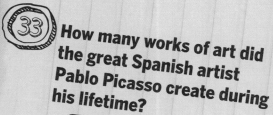

**33** **How many works of art did the great Spanish artist Pablo Picasso create during his lifetime?**

**A.** Roughly 100. The rest of it could hardly be called art.

**B.** Roughly 4,000. That's about one work a week, for 75 years (he actually was an artist that long!).

**C.** Roughly 8,000. OK, he worked evenings and weekends on occasion.

**D.** More than 20,000. Because every multiple-choice question needs one ridiculous answer.

Answers on page 99

### 34. The *Mona Lisa* is considered the world's most popular painting, with more than six million people viewing it each year. How long did it take Leonardo da Vinci to finish painting it?

**A.** An afternoon. A little wine, a little cheese, a little paint, and voila! It's done. That's how genius works.

**B.** A week. Seriously, a work that great takes focus and hard work to get right.

**C.** Two years. You can't rush inspiration. And da Vinci also had a few other things going on at the time, like inventing a flying machine.

**D.** 15 years. But what's 15 years when people are going to be looking at it for the next 600 years?

### 35. What is the Mundi Man?

**A.** The world's biggest work of art

**B.** The name scientists give to the first caveman to make drawings

**C.** A super-tall metal sculpture in Barcelona, Spain

**D.** An amazingly yummy noodle dish from Singapore

## Answers
### From pages 94-95

**28. D.** Aluminum powder sticks to almost everything, including the back of the glass screen. Etch-a-Sketch lines are created by a stylus that "etches" aluminum powder off the screen. Shake the Etch-a-Sketch, and little balls covered with the aluminum powder reapply it to the glass screen.

**29. B.** For hundreds of years, a cartoon wasn't meant to be funny. The modern definition began to emerge in the 1800s.

**30. A.** The sculpture, known as *The Age of Bronze*, was so realistic that many people thought Rodin had used a live person to make it by covering him in bronze and killing him in the process. Of course, it wasn't true.

**31. A.** All these museums are real, but the Museum of Bad Art has the least valuable collection. Its 573 pieces are worth an average of two dollars each, for a total collection value of just over $1,000.

# True or False

**1** Ancient Chinese artists would not show a woman's feet in paintings.

☐ T     ☐ F

**2** The world's largest art gallery is in France.

☐ T     ☐ F

**3** Paintbrushes used to be made out of animal hair, and sometimes still are.

☐ T     ☐ F

**4** Before paint was invented, early humans used charcoal, colored goo from animal organs, and dirt to create art.

☐ T     ☐ F

**5** The youngest professional artist to ever sell a painting was three years old.

☐ T     ☐ F

**6** The colors yellow, orange, and red trigger hunger.

☐ T     ☐ F

Answers on page 149

**7** Salvador Dali, the Spanish artist known for his surreal paintings, was kicked out of art school.

◯ T  ◯ F

**8** Tie-dyed T-shirts were invented in the 1960s by an art teacher whose students wanted an easy project that turned their hands froggy green.

◯ T  ◯ F

**9** Many paintings from ancient Egypt have survived because they were coated with a preservative made from diluted camel mucus.

◯ T  ◯ F

**10** The best way to maintain paintbrushes is to leave them in a jar of water or turpentine.

◯ T  ◯ F

**11** Roughly 40 percent of artwork in major museums is by women.

◯ T  ◯ F

**12** Jackson Pollock made most of his famous paintings by laying a canvas on the floor, and flinging or dripping paint onto it from all sides.

◯ T  ◯ F

# Answers
### From pages 96-97

**32.** **C.** Self-portraits are usually the hardest kind of painting for an artist to sell, but they do them all the time because they need practice and models aren't always available, affordable, or easy to work with.

**33.** **C.** Picasso was incredibly productive. Estimates vary widely, but credible experts say he made at least 20,000 signed paintings, prints, drawings, sculptures, and works of art in other media over his long lifetime.

**34.** **C.** Da Vinci is believed to have done much of the painting of the *Mona Lisa* between 1503 and 1506, but many experts say he continued working on it off and on until his death in 1519.

**35.** **A.** Created by the artist Ando, the Mundi Man is the likeness of a smiling cowboy face and hat, carved on the desert floor in Australia using a tractor. It covers more than five million square yards, and is best seen from an airplane flying 10,000 feet high.

# ACK EXAM 6
## Nature
### Answer the Call of the Wild

**1** You can only see a rainbow if...

- **A.** You are friends with a leprechaun
- **B.** Your back is toward the sun
- **C.** Your front is toward the sun
- **D.** You are the proud owner of a unicorn

**2** What's the hardest part of being a pet octopus?

- **A.** I get sooooooo bored.
- **B.** I get sooooooo hungry.
- **C.** My suckers get stuck to the side of the aquarium. A lot.
- **D.** People talk to me in a weird language. Don't you speak Octopish?

Answers on page 103

**3** **Strawberries have something unique among all fruits. What is it?**

A. They grow along the ground.

B. They make perfect milkshakes (except when a chunk gets stuck in my straw).

C. They appear in more song titles than any other fruit.

D. Their seeds are on the outside.

**4** **Which of these is a real sea creature?**

A. The snoozy salmon

B. The snotty jellyfish

C. The snoring babbadoo

D. Godzilla

# Nature

**5** **What type of food does the Venus flytrap plant eat?**

**A.** Flies and other small insects. Easy.

**B.** Big Macs. They're famous for Mac attacks.

**C.** Whatever kind of food is served on Venus. Earthlings, maybe?

**D.** Rotting fruit. It's kinda disgusting.

**6** **What is in the center of this barrel cactus?**

**A.** Water

**B.** Sand

**C.** A barrel. Am I right?

**D.** A can of tuna fish. It's the weirdest thing. (Actually, we put it in right before we took the photo.)

Answers on page 105

**7** There's something wrong with the following sentence: Blue whales are the largest fish on the planet. What's the error?

A. They're not blue.

B. They're not fish.

C. They're not on the planet. If you're in the ocean, you're "in" the planet, right?

D. All whales, big or small, are blue sometimes. Everyone gets sad now and then.

**8** About 85 percent of all plant life lives where?

A. Under my brother's bed. I've seen it. It's nasty.

B. In the jungles of the world

C. In the ocean

D. On farms. Of course.

## Answers
### From pages 100-101

1. **B.** The right position is key to spotting rainbows: Turn your back to the sun and scan above the horizon into the clouds.

2. **A.** Octopi (that's more than one octopus) are becoming popular as pets because they're intelligent and beautiful. But they get really bored and frustrated when they're confined to an aquarium.

3. **D.** All other fruit carry their seeds on the inside, but strawberries have theirs speckled over the skins.

4. **B.** Snotties get up to five feet across and are the largest of all jellyfish.

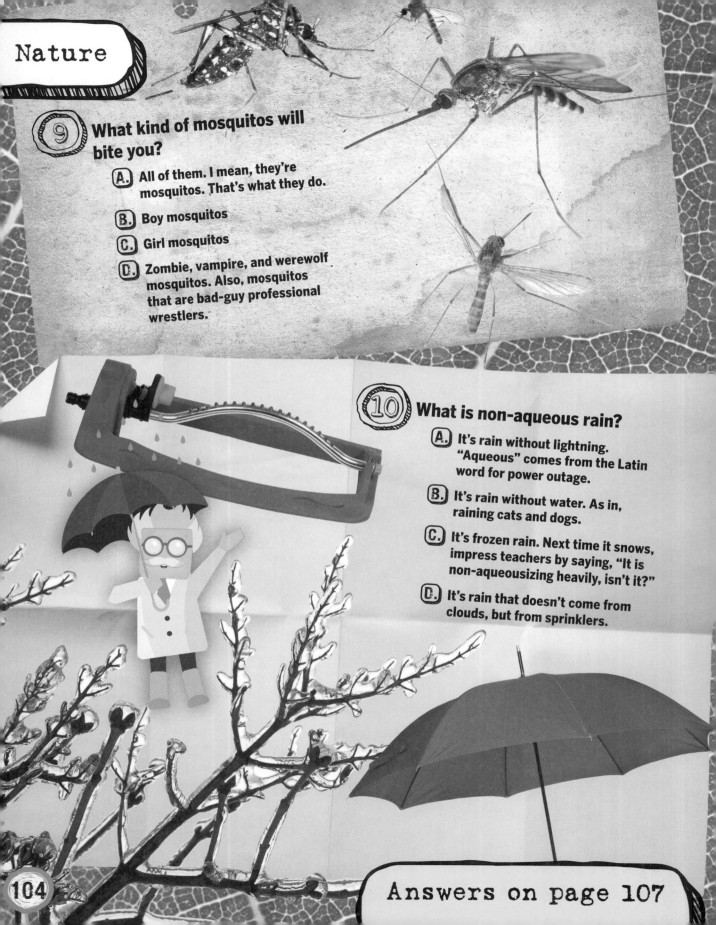

**9** What kind of mosquitos will bite you?

**A.** All of them. I mean, they're mosquitos. That's what they do.

**B.** Boy mosquitos

**C.** Girl mosquitos

**D.** Zombie, vampire, and werewolf mosquitos. Also, mosquitos that are bad-guy professional wrestlers.

**10** What is non-aqueous rain?

**A.** It's rain without lightning. "Aqueous" comes from the Latin word for power outage.

**B.** It's rain without water. As in, raining cats and dogs.

**C.** It's frozen rain. Next time it snows, impress teachers by saying, "It is non-aqueousizing heavily, isn't it?"

**D.** It's rain that doesn't come from clouds, but from sprinklers.

Answers on page 107

## 11 What is St. Elmo's fire?

A. It's a strange kind of lightning.

B. I asked my mom and she says it's a really great movie. Then she started singing a song about a man in motion or something.

C. It's a prayer used when wet wood won't light.

D. It's a fire caused by volcanoes.

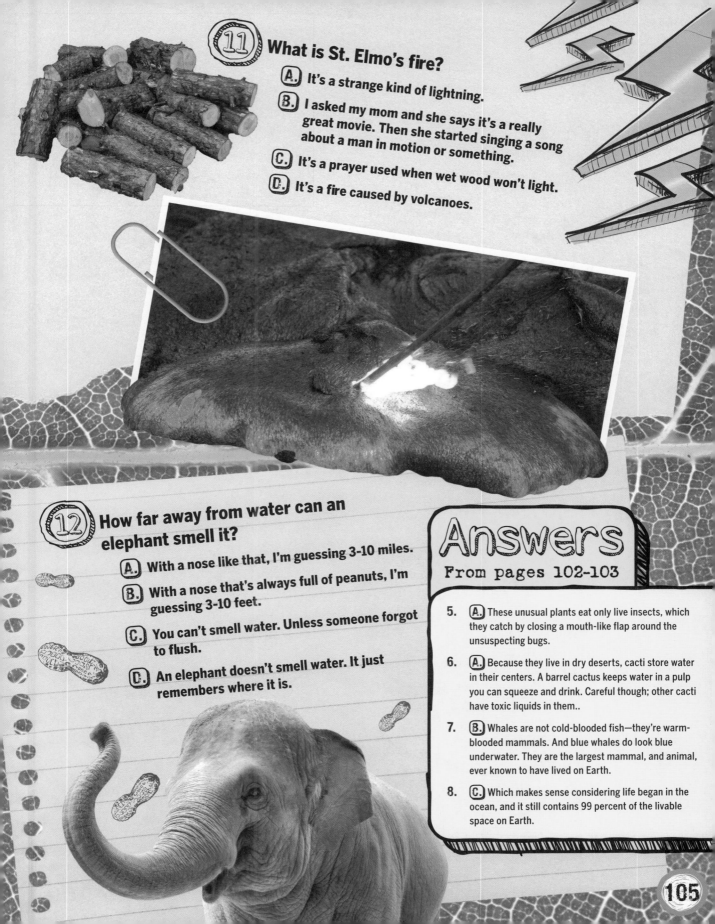

## 12 How far away from water can an elephant smell it?

A. With a nose like that, I'm guessing 3-10 miles.

B. With a nose that's always full of peanuts, I'm guessing 3-10 feet.

C. You can't smell water. Unless someone forgot to flush.

D. An elephant doesn't smell water. It just remembers where it is.

# Answers
## From pages 102-103

5. **A.** These unusual plants eat only live insects, which they catch by closing a mouth-like flap around the unsuspecting bugs.

6. **A.** Because they live in dry deserts, cacti store water in their centers. A barrel cactus keeps water in a pulp you can squeeze and drink. Careful though; other cacti have toxic liquids in them..

7. **B.** Whales are not cold-blooded fish—they're warm-blooded mammals. And blue whales do look blue underwater. They are the largest mammal, and animal, ever known to have lived on Earth.

8. **C.** Which makes sense considering life began in the ocean, and it still contains 99 percent of the livable space on Earth.

# Nature

**13** What kind of animal is this?

A. It's a cutie patootie.

B. It's a badger.

C. It's a squirrel an hour after discovering a 10-pound bag of dog food.

D. It's a wombat.

**14** Which of these is an ability of certain snakes?

A. Flying

B. Being disgusting and slithery and creepy

C. Dancing

D. Speaking Parseltongue, but only with Parselmouths

**15** Which of these is an ability of certain spiders?

A. Is this the disgusting section of the test? Can I skip ahead?

B. Flying

C. Twerking

D. Dancing

Answers on page 109

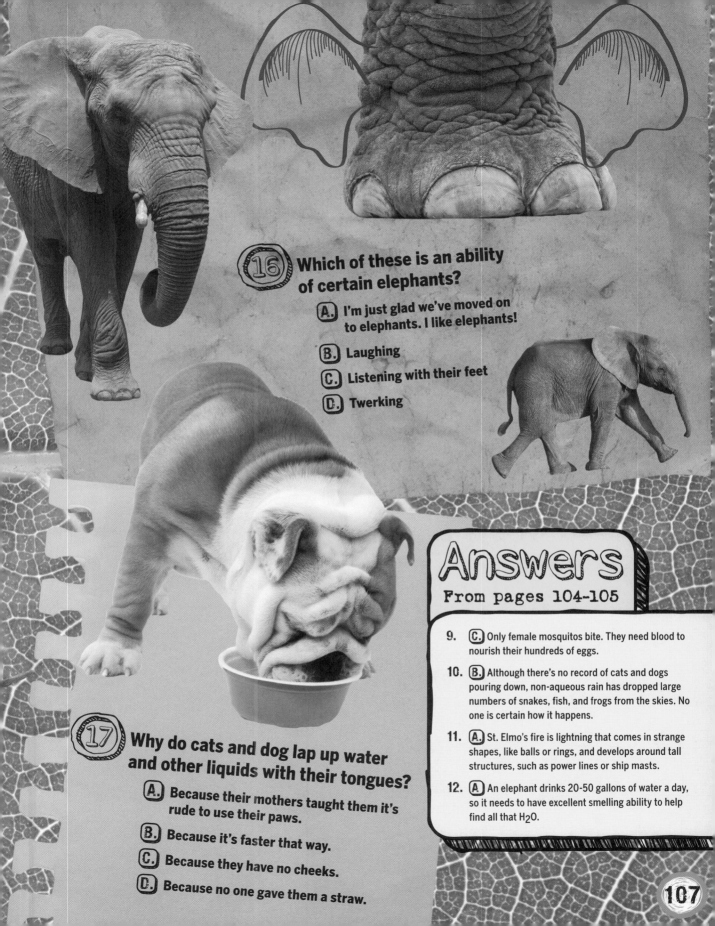

**16.** Which of these is an ability of certain elephants?

A. I'm just glad we've moved on to elephants. I like elephants!

B. Laughing

C. Listening with their feet

D. Twerking

**17.** Why do cats and dog lap up water and other liquids with their tongues?

A. Because their mothers taught them it's rude to use their paws.

B. Because it's faster that way.

C. Because they have no cheeks.

D. Because no one gave them a straw.

## Answers
### From pages 104-105

9. **C.** Only female mosquitos bite. They need blood to nourish their hundreds of eggs.

10. **B.** Although there's no record of cats and dogs pouring down, non-aqueous rain has dropped large numbers of snakes, fish, and frogs from the skies. No one is certain how it happens.

11. **A.** St. Elmo's fire is lightning that comes in strange shapes, like balls or rings, and develops around tall structures, such as power lines or ship masts.

12. **A** An elephant drinks 20-50 gallons of water a day, so it needs to have excellent smelling ability to help find all that $H_2O$.

**18** **What is happening today to the world's oldest and biggest trees?**

A. They're dying much faster than they used to.

B. They're growing much taller than they used to.

C. They're being turned into tree houses.

D. They're learning to walk.

**19** **How much carbon dioxide can a tree absorb over its lifetime?**

A. Measured by volume, I would say...a lot.

B. Measured by weight, I would say 2,000 pounds.

C. Measured by molecules, I would say about 3.8 gazillion.

D. Measured by human exhalations, I would say a soccer stadium.

Answers on page 111

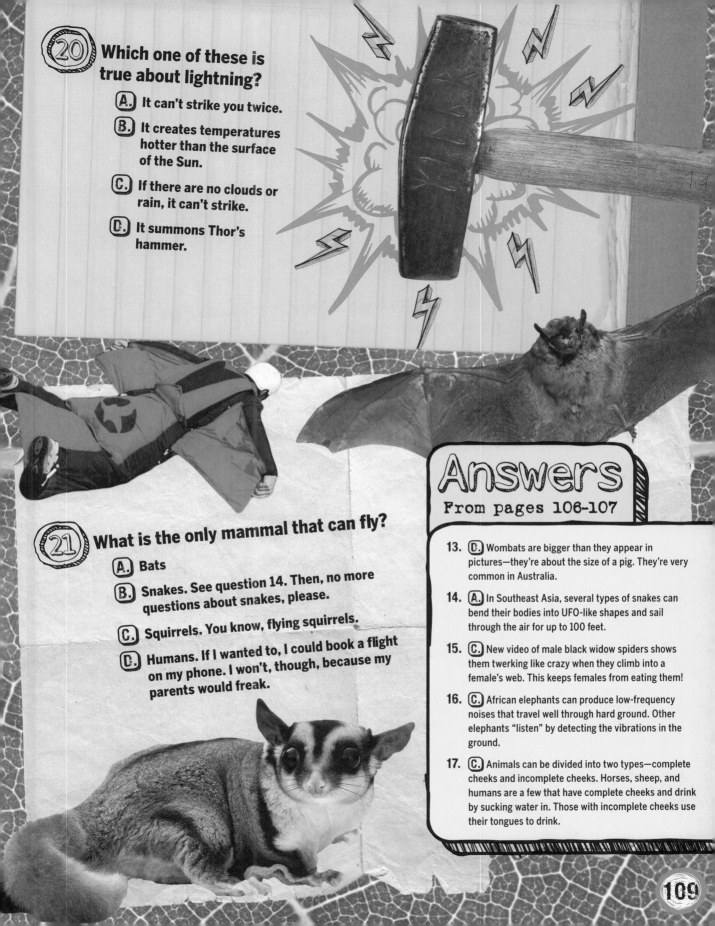

**20** Which one of these is true about lightning?

**A.** It can't strike you twice.

**B.** It creates temperatures hotter than the surface of the Sun.

**C.** If there are no clouds or rain, it can't strike.

**D.** It summons Thor's hammer.

**21** What is the only mammal that can fly?

**A.** Bats

**B.** Snakes. See question 14. Then, no more questions about snakes, please.

**C.** Squirrels. You know, flying squirrels.

**D.** Humans. If I wanted to, I could book a flight on my phone. I won't, though, because my parents would freak.

## Answers
### From pages 106-107

13. **D.** Wombats are bigger than they appear in pictures—they're about the size of a pig. They're very common in Australia.

14. **A.** In Southeast Asia, several types of snakes can bend their bodies into UFO-like shapes and sail through the air for up to 100 feet.

15. **C.** New video of male black widow spiders shows them twerking like crazy when they climb into a female's web. This keeps females from eating them!

16. **C.** African elephants can produce low-frequency noises that travel well through hard ground. Other elephants "listen" by detecting the vibrations in the ground.

17. **C.** Animals can be divided into two types—complete cheeks and incomplete cheeks. Horses, sheep, and humans are a few that have complete cheeks and drink by sucking water in. Those with incomplete cheeks use their tongues to drink.

# Nature

**22. What can a snake do with its eyelids closed?**

A. I JUST SAID, NO MORE SNAKES!

B. See you

C. Hear you

D. Drive a little snake car. The snake police aren't too happy when they do this.

**23. Hummingbirds are the only bird that can do this.**

A. Hum. That's why they're called hummingbirds.

B. Fly backward

C. Fly faster than a sports car

D. Spit watermelon seeds

**24. Why does your dog yowl and howl when an ambulance blaring its siren goes by?**

A. He wants to chase it. Oh so badly. Let me out!

B. He's saying, "An ambulance is going by, somebody got hurt" in dog language.

C. It hurts his ears.

D. He's spreading the word to other dogs.

Answers on page 113

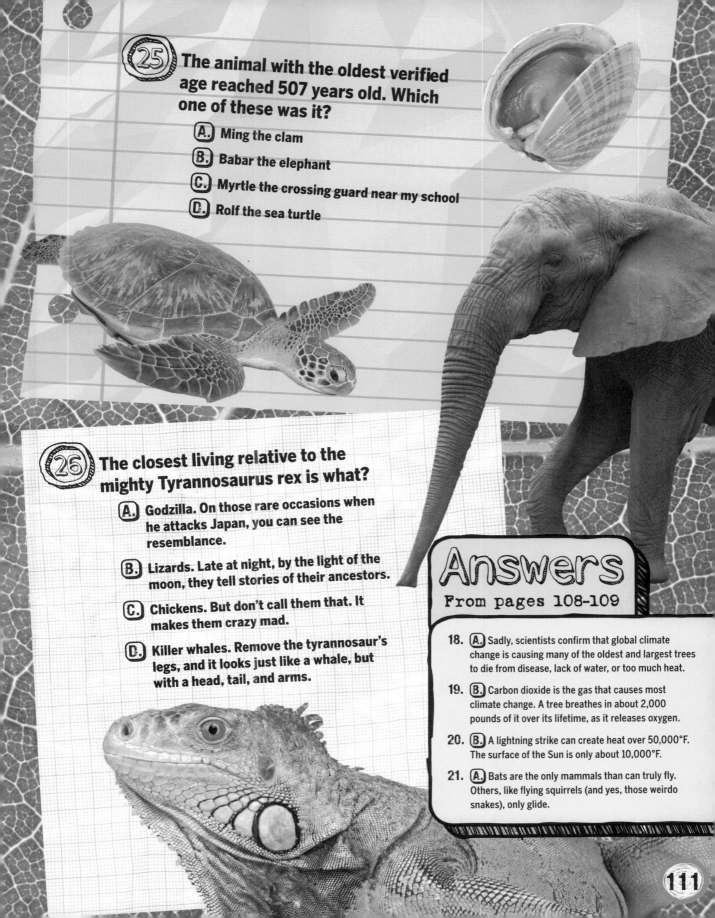

**25** The animal with the oldest verified age reached 507 years old. Which one of these was it?

- **A.** Ming the clam
- **B.** Babar the elephant
- **C.** Myrtle the crossing guard near my school
- **D.** Rolf the sea turtle

**26** The closest living relative to the mighty Tyrannosaurus rex is what?

- **A.** Godzilla. On those rare occasions when he attacks Japan, you can see the resemblance.
- **B.** Lizards. Late at night, by the light of the moon, they tell stories of their ancestors.
- **C.** Chickens. But don't call them that. It makes them crazy mad.
- **D.** Killer whales. Remove the tyrannosaur's legs, and it looks just like a whale, but with a head, tail, and arms.

## Answers
### From pages 108-109

18. **A.** Sadly, scientists confirm that global climate change is causing many of the oldest and largest trees to die from disease, lack of water, or too much heat.

19. **B.** Carbon dioxide is the gas that causes most climate change. A tree breathes in about 2,000 pounds of it over its lifetime, as it releases oxygen.

20. **B.** A lightning strike can create heat over 50,000°F. The surface of the Sun is only about 10,000°F.

21. **A.** Bats are the only mammals than can truly fly. Others, like flying squirrels (and yes, those weirdo snakes), only glide.

**27** Which of these lays the biggest eggs?

A. Chickens. Again with the chickens? Move on already.

B. Comedians. They tell jokes, no one laughs, Dad says, "He just laid a giant egg!"

C. Sharks

D. Ostriches

**28** Beavers have to keep chewing all the time or else what would happen?

A. They would have to talk to each other.

B. Their tails would fall off and they'd turn into groundhogs.

C. Forests would get overpopulated with trees.

D. Their teeth would grow out of control.

Answers on page 115

**29** **If you give a mama rat and a papa rat 18 months to grow a family, how many rat descendants could they have at the end?**

**A.** One million. Someone bring me a cat army!

**B.** One thousand. Their kids have kids, their grandkids have kids, soon you need to rent a party center to have a decent family get-together.

**C.** One hundred. Someone bring me a lab coat and a maze!

**D.** We don't even know if they want kids right now. They might be focused on their careers, you know.

**30** **What color is a polar bear's skin?**

**A.** White

**B.** Black

**C.** It's all polka dots. Don't mention it though—they're embarrassed by it.

**D.** Pink. You know, underneath that fur is just a nice mammal like you and me.

## Answers
### From pages 110-111

22. **B.** Snakes have clear eyelids that are fused together. This eye cap is called a brille and it protects snakes' eyes from dust and dirt, but lets them see.

23. **B.** Hummingbirds beat their wings up to 80 times per second! This allows them to hover, fly sideways, and even go backward.

24. **D.** When dogs hunted in packs like wolves, they howled to spread the word that a chase was on. And a siren sounds to them like another dog running and howling.

25. **A.** Ming was an ocean quahog clam found off the coast of Iceland in 2006. There are probably clams even older still in the water.

26. **C.** Although tyrannosaurs have been extinct for millions of years, scientists studying their fossils discovered their skeletons were very similar to the bones of modern chickens!

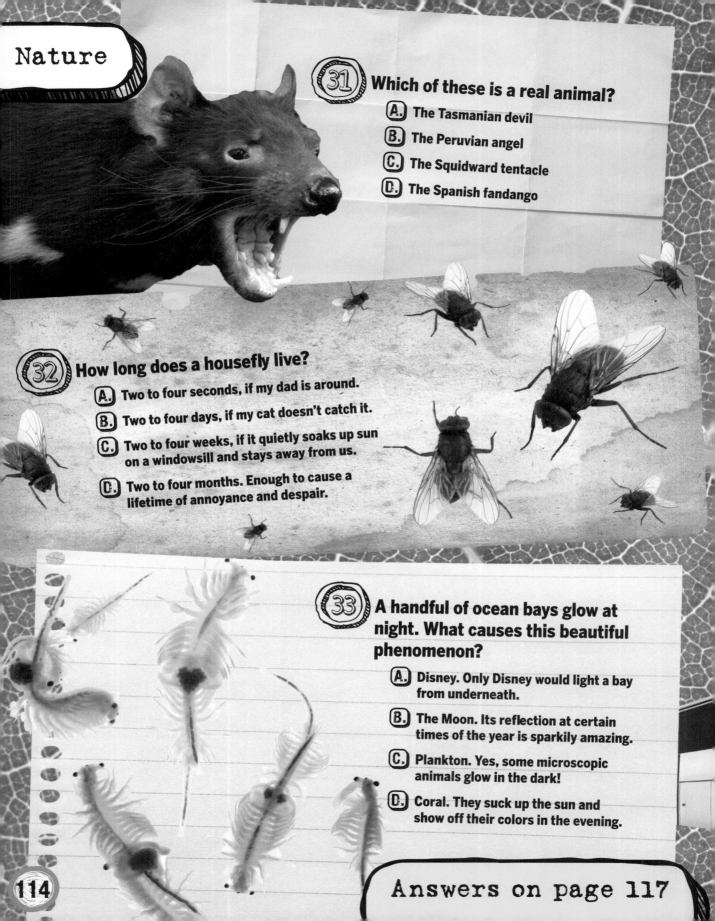

# Nature

**31** Which of these is a real animal?

- **A.** The Tasmanian devil
- **B.** The Peruvian angel
- **C.** The Squidward tentacle
- **D.** The Spanish fandango

**32** How long does a housefly live?

- **A.** Two to four seconds, if my dad is around.
- **B.** Two to four days, if my cat doesn't catch it.
- **C.** Two to four weeks, if it quietly soaks up sun on a windowsill and stays away from us.
- **D.** Two to four months. Enough to cause a lifetime of annoyance and despair.

**33** A handful of ocean bays glow at night. What causes this beautiful phenomenon?

- **A.** Disney. Only Disney would light a bay from underneath.
- **B.** The Moon. Its reflection at certain times of the year is sparkily amazing.
- **C.** Plankton. Yes, some microscopic animals glow in the dark!
- **D.** Coral. They suck up the sun and show off their colors in the evening.

Answers on page 117

**34** What is unusual about the way horses and cows sleep?

A. They prefer harder pillows than most other animals.

B. They can do it standing up.

C. They dream about cow fairies, horse elves, and a world of evil villains and noble heroes.

D. They move in large sleepwalking groups to protect themselves from predators.

**35** An ostrich, a greyhound, a kangaroo, and a rabbit decide to race each other in a 100-yard dash. Assuming they run straight and try hard, who would win?

A. The ostrich. That's because the other animals fall over laughing, watching it waddle.

B. The greyhound. A bus can go fast if it's not packed with riders.

C. The kangaroo. A few hops and it's time for a victory lap.

D. The rabbit. Nothing moves as fast as a rabbit that doesn't want to be eaten.

## Answers
### From pages 112-113

27. C. Surprising, huh? With eggs over a foot in diameter, whale sharks lay the largest eggs in the world!

28. D. Beavers' teeth never, ever stop growing. The dam-builders must chew constantly or their choppers would get so large they could actually kill the beavers!

29. A. Yes, one million! Rats have many babies, and those babies grow quickly and have more babies. Fortunately, lots of other animals eat rats or they'd be everywhere.

30. B. Although its fur is white, a polar bear's skin is black.

# True or False

**1** Crocodiles can climb trees.

◯ T  ◯ F

**2** Aspirin comes from willow trees.

◯ T  ◯ F

**3** Rain contains vitamins.

◯ T  ◯ F

**4** Water lilies can be six feet across.

◯ T  ◯ F

**5** Sharks have the most bones of any fish.

◯ T  ◯ F

**6** Giraffes have four stomachs.

◯ T  ◯ F

**7** Penguins only live in Antarctica.

◯ T  ◯ F

Answers on page 149

**8** Cheetahs are the only big cats that can't roar.

◻ T    ◻ F

**9** Male ostriches are the only big birds that can roar.

◻ T    ◻ F

**10** Frogs can drink the water they live in.

◻ T    ◻ F

**11** Flamingoes can only eat if their head is upside down.

◻ T    ◻ F

**12** A snail can sleep for three years.

◻ T    ◻ F

**13** The telegraph plant can send messages long distances through the air.

◻ T    ◻ F

**14** Archerfish hunt by spitting at their prey.

◻ T    ◻ F

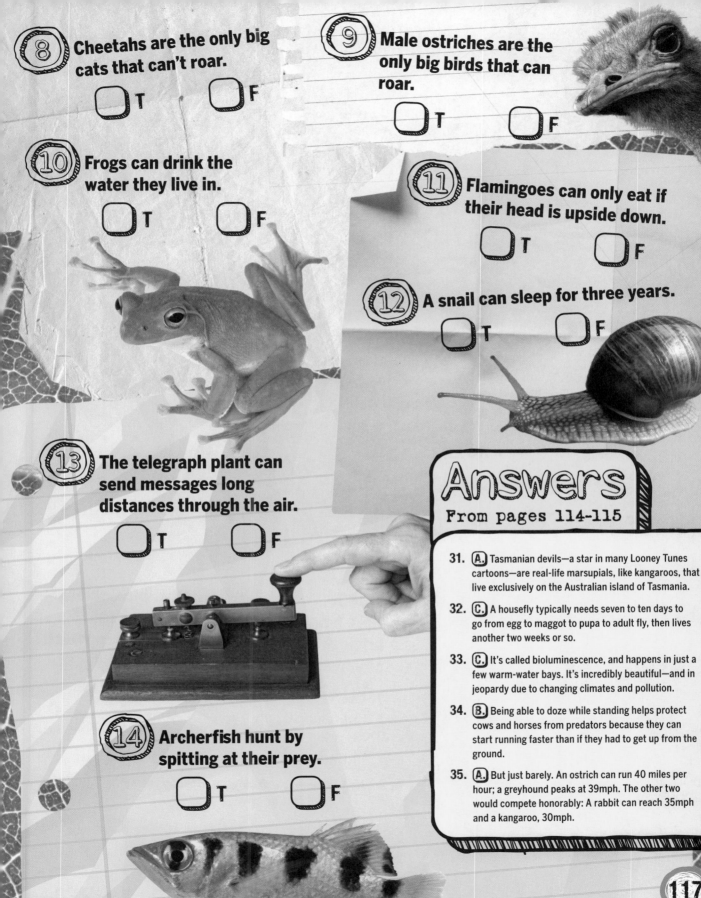

## Answers
### From pages 114–115

**31.** **A.** Tasmanian devils—a star in many Looney Tunes cartoons—are real-life marsupials, like kangaroos, that live exclusively on the Australian island of Tasmania.

**32.** **C.** A housefly typically needs seven to ten days to go from egg to maggot to pupa to adult fly, then lives another two weeks or so.

**33.** **C.** It's called bioluminescence, and happens in just a few warm-water bays. It's incredibly beautiful—and in jeopardy due to changing climates and pollution.

**34.** **B.** Being able to doze while standing helps protect cows and horses from predators because they can start running faster than if they had to get up from the ground.

**35.** **A.** But just barely. An ostrich can run 40 miles per hour; a greyhound peaks at 39mph. The other two would compete honorably: A rabbit can reach 35mph and a kangaroo, 30mph.

117

# History

## Why Does It Repeat Itself?
## We said, WHY Does It Repeat Itself?

**1** **Who invented pasta?**

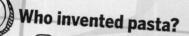

**A.** Marco Polo. The explorer, not the game.

**B.** Someone in China

**C.** The Monks of La Pasta, a small monastery in southern Italy long since abandoned

**D.** Alphonso Dente. You can call him Al.

**2** **In 1896, the first modern Olympic Games were held, an event not seen since the original Olympics 1,500 years earlier. Which city hosted the 1896 return of the Games?**

**A.** London, England

**B.** It wasn't a city. They set up tents for a three-day competition on a farm in Italy called Woodstockius.

**C.** Athens, Greece

**D.** Olympia, Washington. How do you think the city got its name?

Answers on page 121

**3** Which of these did the Roman emperor Caligula promise to appoint as consul, a political office in ancient Rome second in power only to the emperor himself?

A. His horse, Incitatus

B. A statue of himself

C. Malcolm McDowell, the actor who played him in the movie *Caligula*

D. Ben Franklin

**4** Where did Christopher Columbus land on his 1492 voyage across the Atlantic Ocean?

A. Plymouth Rock, wasn't it? They quickly built a shopping mall, and the rest is history.

B. The Bahamas. Hey, maybe he was the first to vacation in the Caribbean!

C. The earth was flat back then. He sailed right into the fence along the edge, threw a few pebbles over for fun, then turned back.

D. Somewhere near Miami, Florida.

**5** This building was completed about 2,000 years ago by a man named Titus. What is it called?

A. Titan. It's named after Titus.

B. The Coliseum, also spelled Colosseum. It's named after Titus's dog, Colossus.

C. The Royal Athens Opera House

D. The Globe Theatre. It's where Shakespeare worked.

**6** What did ancient Egyptians use for pillows?

A. Cats. Which was more comfortable and less wiggly than it sounds.

B. Stone. Super easy to find in Egypt.

C. Pyramid workers. But only the ones who got too soft to keep building pyramids.

D. Hay. Super hard to find in Egypt.

**7** Who was the T-shirt invented for in 1904?

A. For unmarried men who couldn't sew loose buttons.

B. For movie stars who wanted to look tough and cool.

C. For plumbers, to cover their you-know-whats when they bent down too low.

D. For fans of the singing group sensation of that time, the Dusty Trail Boys.

**8** The United States declared independence from Great Britain in 1776. What was its first capital city?

A. Philadelphia

B. Washington, D.C.

C. Sheboygan

D. Hollywood

Answers on page 123

**9** **What is the name of this painting by Leonardo da Vinci?**

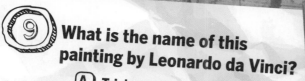

**A.** Trick question. Leonardo was a ninja turtle, not a painter!

**B.** How did a question from the Art section get over here?

**C.** *The Mona Lisa*

**D.** *Venus de Milo*

**10** **The Lisa lady in the painting doesn't have eyebrows. Any thoughts on why?**

**A.** Shhhhh! She's very sensitive about it.

**B.** People didn't have them 500 years ago—eyebrows were invented in 1904 to go with T-shirts.

**C.** What's considered beautiful changes throughout history.

**D.** It was a time when eyebrows carried disease so people shaved them off.

# Answers
### From pages 118-119

1. **A.** Marco Polo, an Italian explorer, didn't invent pasta but he spread the word. He brought pasta-making techniques home from China in the year 1271.

2. **C.** The ancient Olympics started in Greece, and so did the modern Games.

3. **A.** Caligula thought so highly of his horse that he gave Incitatus servants, a stable made of marble, a collar made of jewels, and a manger made of ivory. Oh, and Incitatus also ate oats topped with flakes of gold!

4. **B.** Columbus landed among the many islands of the Bahamas, probably on the one now known as San Salvador Island.

5. **B.** Emperor Titus Flavius ruled the Roman Empire when the Coliseum was finished in 80 A.D. The word coliseum comes from colossal, meaning gigantic.

## 11 What's the Renaissance?

A. That's Italian for "rainy season."

B. A time when democracies first started to form

C. It's when people dress up in costumes from ye days of olde and say things like "forsooth" and "alack."

D. A period of great intellectual and cultural advances

## 12 Before alarms clocks, how did English and Irish people get to work on time?

A. Roosters. All those cock-a-doodle-doos made whole cities sound like giant farmyards.

B. Moms. All those "get-up-or-you're-going-to-be-lates" made whole cities sound like my house.

C. They'd hire people to bang on their doors.

D. They checked their sundials.

## 13 Built for a fair in 1889, this metal structure in Paris, France, was only supposed to stay up for 20 years. What's it called?

A. The Eiffel Tower

B. The 20-Year Tower

C. The Lego Tower

D. The Hilton Tower. How do you think Paris Hilton got her name?

Answers on page 125

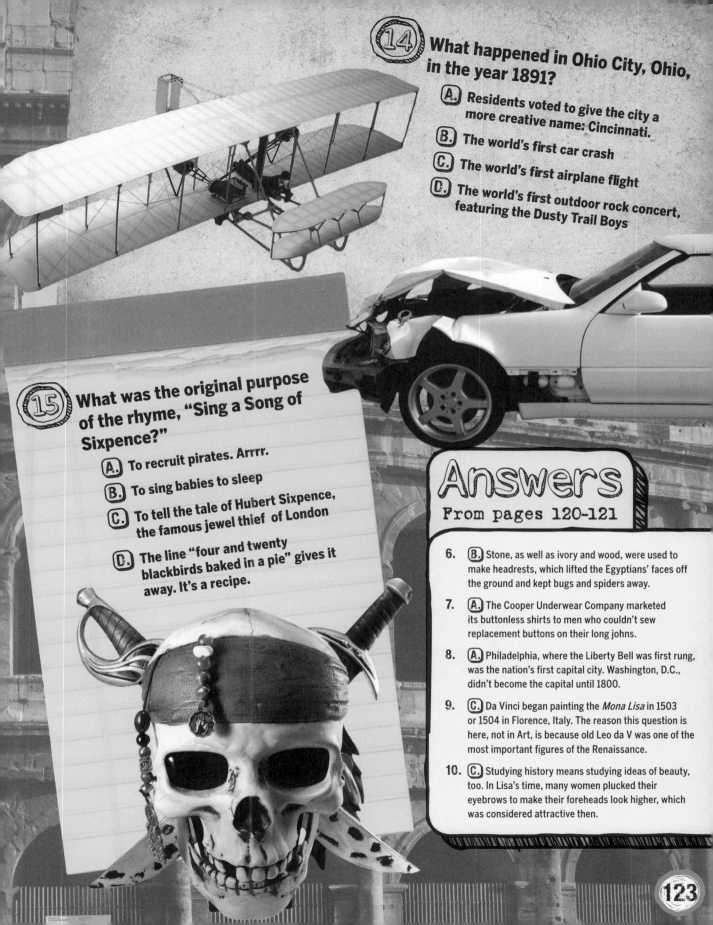

**14** **What happened in Ohio City, Ohio, in the year 1891?**

**A.** Residents voted to give the city a more creative name: Cincinnati.

**B.** The world's first car crash

**C.** The world's first airplane flight

**D.** The world's first outdoor rock concert, featuring the Dusty Trail Boys

**15** **What was the original purpose of the rhyme, "Sing a Song of Sixpence?"**

**A.** To recruit pirates. Arrrr.

**B.** To sing babies to sleep

**C.** To tell the tale of Hubert Sixpence, the famous jewel thief of London

**D.** The line "four and twenty blackbirds baked in a pie" gives it away. It's a recipe.

## Answers
### From pages 120-121

6. **B.** Stone, as well as ivory and wood, were used to make headrests, which lifted the Egyptians' faces off the ground and kept bugs and spiders away.

7. **A.** The Cooper Underwear Company marketed its buttonless shirts to men who couldn't sew replacement buttons on their long johns.

8. **A.** Philadelphia, where the Liberty Bell was first rung, was the nation's first capital city. Washington, D.C., didn't become the capital until 1800.

9. **C.** Da Vinci began painting the *Mona Lisa* in 1503 or 1504 in Florence, Italy. The reason this question is here, not in Art, is because old Leo da V was one of the most important figures of the Renaissance.

10. **C.** Studying history means studying ideas of beauty, too. In Lisa's time, many women plucked their eyebrows to make their foreheads look higher, which was considered attractive then.

**16** Why did pirates wear eye patches?

**A.** Because their parrots couldn't recognize them otherwise.

**B.** Because they were blind in that eye. Duhhh.

**C.** Because it was so dark below decks.

**D.** Because it made them look mean and tough.

**17** Who invented paper?

**A.** People in China in the second century B.C. It was cheaper than writing on silk.

**B.** A man in Germany in the 1500s. He used it to post a notice on a church door about a lost cat.

**C.** British schoolkids in the 1800s. They wanted it for paper airplanes because slate airplanes flew terribly and shattered on impact.

**D.** Cavemen in 10,000 B.C., right after inventing the wheel. The paper was used to write speeding tickets to fast wheelers.

**18** Where was toilet paper first used?

**A.** Uh...in a bathroom, I hope

**B.** In Russia, to decorate the homes of people who had done something really stupid

**C.** In ancient China

**D.** In ancient Porcelain

Answers on page 127

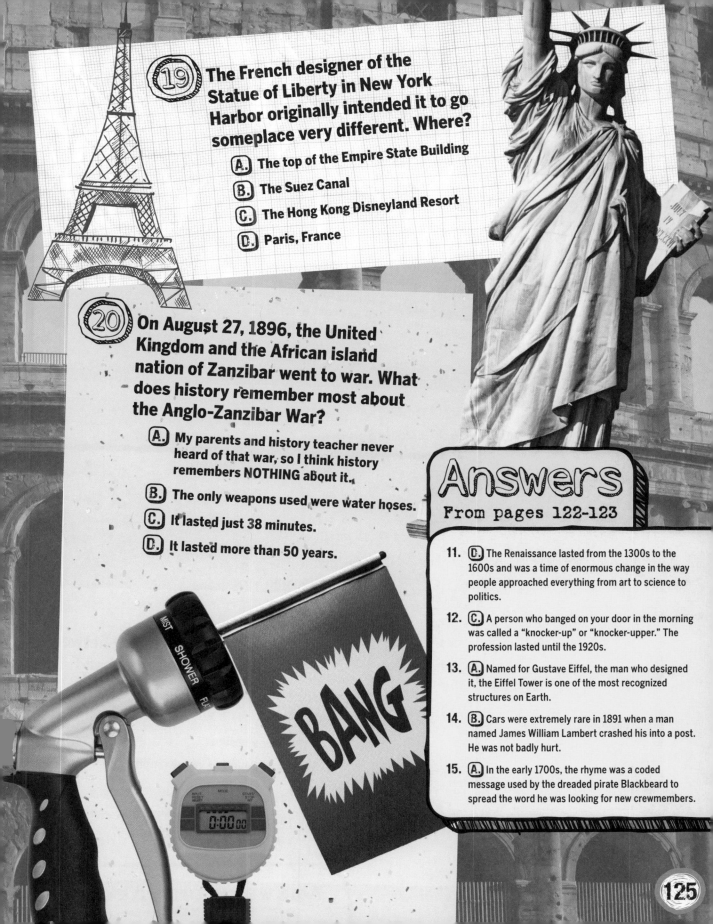

**19** The French designer of the Statue of Liberty in New York Harbor originally intended it to go someplace very different. Where?

A. The top of the Empire State Building

B. The Suez Canal

C. The Hong Kong Disneyland Resort

D. Paris, France

**20** On August 27, 1896, the United Kingdom and the African island nation of Zanzibar went to war. What does history remember most about the Anglo-Zanzibar War?

A. My parents and history teacher never heard of that war, so I think history remembers NOTHING about it.

B. The only weapons used were water hoses.

C. It lasted just 38 minutes.

D. It lasted more than 50 years.

BANG

## Answers

From pages 122-123

11. **C.** The Renaissance lasted from the 1300s to the 1600s and was a time of enormous change in the way people approached everything from art to science to politics.

12. **C.** A person who banged on your door in the morning was called a "knocker-up" or "knocker-upper." The profession lasted until the 1920s.

13. **A.** Named for Gustave Eiffel, the man who designed it, the Eiffel Tower is one of the most recognized structures on Earth.

14. **B.** Cars were extremely rare in 1891 when a man named James William Lambert crashed his into a post. He was not badly hurt.

15. **A.** In the early 1700s, the rhyme was a coded message used by the dreaded pirate Blackbeard to spread the word he was looking for new crewmembers.

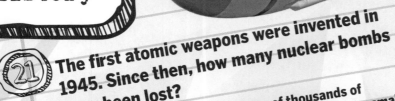

**21.** The first atomic weapons were invented in 1945. Since then, how many nuclear bombs have been lost?

**A.** 50-100. Hey, there are tens of thousands of nuclear bombs out there; you gotta expect a small percentage to get lost!

**B.** 6. They're together on the floor of the Atlantic Ocean, in one giant cargo bin.

**C.** 2. Scientists believe the lovebirds ran off together and are living in disguise on a tropical island.

**D.** 0. Seriously, how do you lose a NUCLEAR BOMB? It's not like forgetting where you put your glasses or anything.

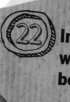

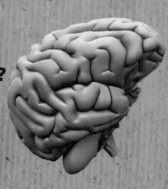

**22.** In the Middle Ages, what did people who studied medicine and anatomy believe was the center of intelligence?

**A.** The heart

**B.** The brain

**C.** The Central Intelligence Agency

**D.** That itchy spot between your shoulder blades you can't reach with either hand

**23.** During the Hundred Years War between England and France, a certain hand gesture was used for the first time. Which one?

**A.** The peace sign

**B.** Are you talking about flipping the bird? Cool!

**C.** The loser 'L'

**D.** The finger gun. As in, "I'm pretending to shoot you with my finger and thumb."

Answers on page 129

**24** Andrew Jackson, the seventh president of the United States, died in 1845. At his funeral, Jackson's pet parrot was taken outside. Why?

&#$%

A. The poor thing was overcome with grief and needed some fresh air.

B. Jackson's last wish was that it be set free.

C. There was a meteorite shower the parrot wanted to see.

D. It kept swearing.

**25** Attila the Hun was one of history's most feared conquerors. Before he died in 453, his empire stretched across Europe into Asia. How did he die?

A. With glory, on the battlefield, defending his empire

B. In a prison in Germany, after he got arrested for letting his horse do its duty in the middle of the road

C. From a nosebleed

D. From a heart attack

## Answers
### From pages 124-125

16. **C.** Going from bright sun into darkness below caused temporary night blindness, so many pirates kept one eye covered to keep it adjusted to the dark.

17. **A.** Until paper was invented, the Chinese wrote on expensive silk cloth.

18. **C.** Since the Chinese invented paper, it's only natural they were the first to go down below with it.

19. **B.** Sculptor Frederic Auguste Bartholdi designed the statue for the entrance of Egypt's Suez Canal. The plan called for a giant lighthouse in the shape of an Egyptian woman wrapped in traditional robes and holding a torch. It was never built and he modified the design slightly for Lady Liberty.

20. **C.** The first shots were fired at 9:02 a.m., and the last ones stopped at 9:40 a.m. after Zanzibar's sultan fled his palace. It was the shortest war in history.

## 26. Which of these has been used most for chronicling history?

A. The iPhone, but only the 4s model. The 5s just never took hold.

B. The quill pen

C. The typewriter

D. The hammer and chisel

## 27. What was the Magna Carta?

A. The menu of food choices on the first ships that crossed the Atlantic Ocean

B. The beginning of the modern legal system

C. I think magna means big and carta means map. So the Magna Carta is a Big Map.

D. It was the beginning of democracy.

## 28. Which was the first famous book to be typed on a typewriter?

A. *The Adventures of Tom Sawyer*, by Mark Twain

B. *The Typewriter Manual*, First Edition

C. *The Holy Bible*, Helvetica Edition

D. *Walden*, by Henry David Thoreau

Answers on page 131

**29** In 1883, a train service began that would live in the imaginations of travelers for the next century. By connecting the cities of Paris and Constantinople (now called Istanbul), it also connected two continents—Europe and Asia. What was it called?

**A.** The Love Train

**B.** The Marco Polo Train (not game)

**C.** The Trans-Siberian Express

**D.** The Orient Express

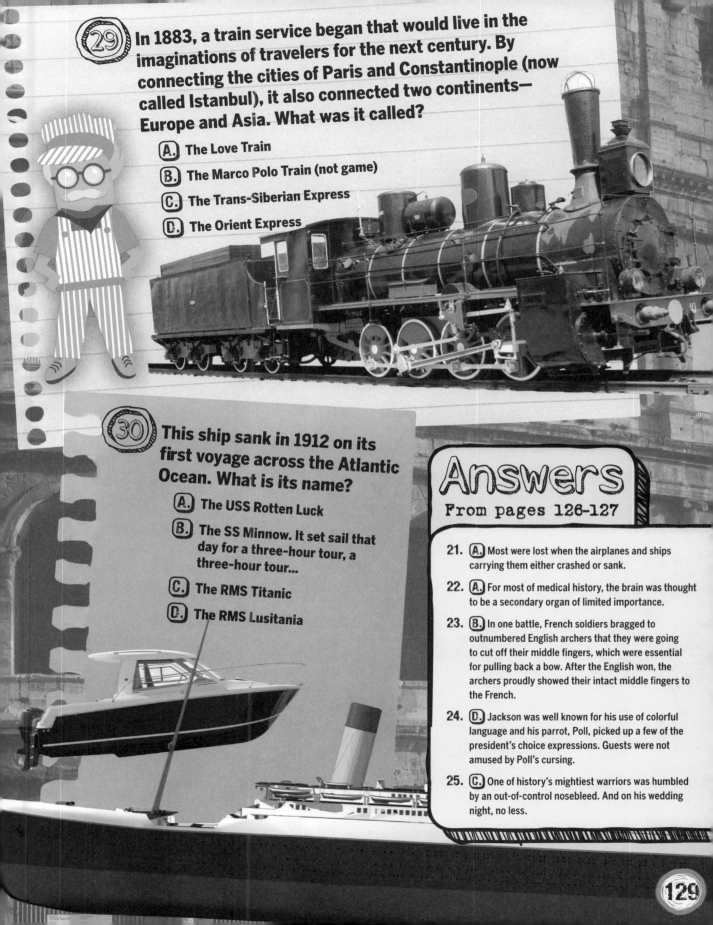

**30** This ship sank in 1912 on its first voyage across the Atlantic Ocean. What is its name?

**A.** The USS Rotten Luck

**B.** The SS Minnow. It set sail that day for a three-hour tour, a three-hour tour...

**C.** The RMS Titanic

**D.** The RMS Lusitania

## Answers
### From pages 126-127

21. **A.** Most were lost when the airplanes and ships carrying them either crashed or sank.

22. **A.** For most of medical history, the brain was thought to be a secondary organ of limited importance.

23. **B.** In one battle, French soldiers bragged to outnumbered English archers that they were going to cut off their middle fingers, which were essential for pulling back a bow. After the English won, the archers proudly showed their intact middle fingers to the French.

24. **D.** Jackson was well known for his use of colorful language and his parrot, Poll, picked up a few of the president's choice expressions. Guests were not amused by Poll's cursing.

25. **C.** One of history's mightiest warriors was humbled by an out-of-control nosebleed. And on his wedding night, no less.

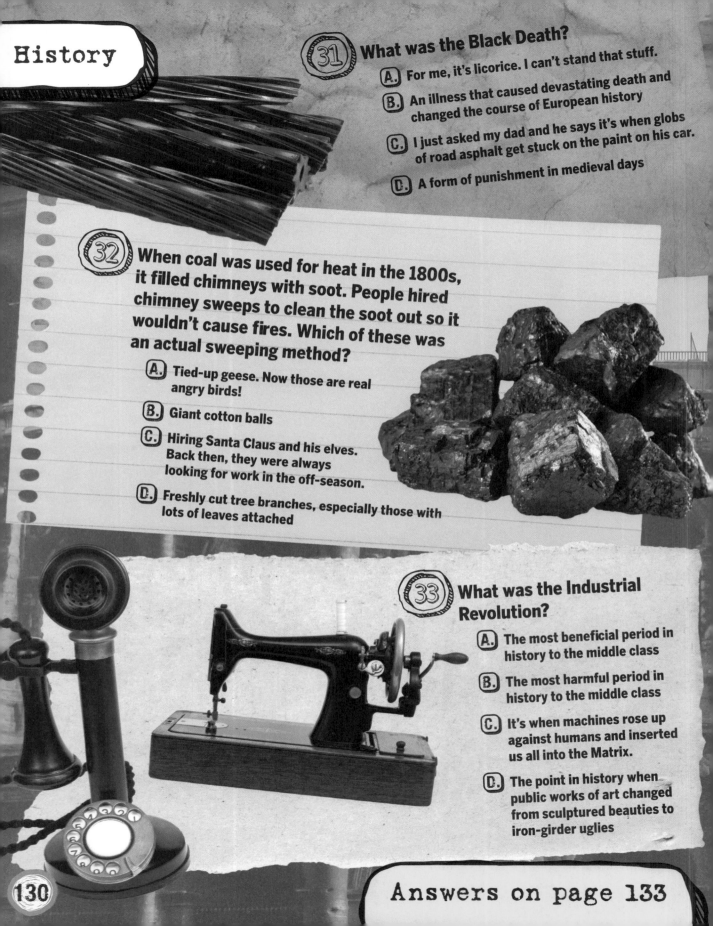

**31** **What was the Black Death?**

A. For me, it's licorice. I can't stand that stuff.

B. An illness that caused devastating death and changed the course of European history

C. I just asked my dad and he says it's when globs of road asphalt get stuck on the paint on his car.

D. A form of punishment in medieval days

**32** **When coal was used for heat in the 1800s, it filled chimneys with soot. People hired chimney sweeps to clean the soot out so it wouldn't cause fires. Which of these was an actual sweeping method?**

A. Tied-up geese. Now those are real angry birds!

B. Giant cotton balls

C. Hiring Santa Claus and his elves. Back then, they were always looking for work in the off-season.

D. Freshly cut tree branches, especially those with lots of leaves attached

**33** **What was the Industrial Revolution?**

A. The most beneficial period in history to the middle class

B. The most harmful period in history to the middle class

C. It's when machines rose up against humans and inserted us all into the Matrix.

D. The point in history when public works of art changed from sculptured beauties to iron-girder uglies

Answers on page 133

**34** Just 100 years ago, average life expectancy was 25-30 years. Now, most people live to age 70 or more. What's the main reason for this?

**A.** Well, for starters, there aren't furious geese looking for revenge any more. That's gotta help.

**B.** Flintstones multivitamins. And broccoli.

**C.** Better education

**D.** More kids are making it to adulthood.

**35** Modern humans first appeared about 200,000 years ago. How much of what took place from then to now is recorded as written history?

**A.** All of it. Well, almost all of it. A few things got left out when historians took time off to attend conferences in Rome and Tokyo.

**B.** About three percent

**C.** About 50 percent

**D.** None of it. History repeats itself because no one was listening the first time.

## Answers
### From pages 128-129

26. **B.** Usually made from goose feathers, quill pens were the primary writing instrument from the sixth to the nineteenth century. They were used to write most of the world's greatest documents, including the Declaration of Independence and the Magna Carta.

27. **B.** Signed by King John of England in 1215, the Magna Carta was the first time an English king agreed to limit his own powers and follow new laws instead. The legal system still used in the Western world today was born with this important document.

28. **A.** Samuel Clemens, who usually wrote under the name Mark Twain, bought his first typewriter in 1874. He turned in the typewritten manuscript for *The Adventures of Tom Sawyer* in the next year.

29. **D.** Known for luxury and romance, The Orient Express lasted until 1977. It has appeared in many books and movies, including Agatha Christie's *Murder on the Orient Express.*

30. **C.** The Titanic was called "unsinkable" because it had 16 watertight sections below decks—and four could be flooded without causing the ship to sink. But when it hit an iceberg, five sections filled with water. Only 700 of the 2,200 passengers survived.

# True or False

**1** A man named Thomas Crapper invented the toilet.

☐ T    ☐ F

**2** In ancient China, doctors only got paid if patients got better.

☐ T    ☐ F

**3** The French emperor Napoleon Bonaparte was really short.

☐ T    ☐ F

**4** Only two people signed the U.S. Declaration of Independence on July 4, 1776.

☐ T    ☐ F

**5** Winnie the Pooh was a real bear.

☐ T    ☐ F

**6** There's a fire in Iraq that has been burning for more than 4,000 years.

☐ T    ☐ F

Answers on pages 149-150

**7** Alexander the Great conquered almost half the civilized world by the time he was 30 years old.

☐ T        ☐ F

**8** Moby Dick was a real whale.

☐ T        ☐ F

**9** The ancient Greek civilization lasted longer than any other in history.

☐ T        ☐ F

**10** The history of China developed mostly independently from the western world because no one understood the languages spoken there.

☐ T        ☐ F

**11** The oldest religion in the world still being practiced today is Judaism.

☐ T        ☐ F

**12** The pyramids in Egypt were built by slaves.

☐ T        ☐ F

# Answers

### From pages 130–131

31. **B.** The Black Death was bubonic plague, a disease that killed up to 60 percent of the people in Europe in the mid-1300s. Its devastating effects changed history for hundreds of years.

32. **A.** With chimneys about 14 inches wide, a goose fit perfectly. Sweeps would tie its legs together and run the indignant bird through the chimney a few times so its flapping would knock off the soot.

33. **A.** The Industrial Revolution was perhaps the most important time in history for moving people out of poverty. The changeover from muscle power to machine power in the late 1700s allowed enormous numbers of people to find high-paying work that moved them into the middle class.

34. **C.** Until recently, the world was a very dangerous place for young people. Dangerous conditions for childbirth, starvation, childhood diseases, and accidents were very common. So remember: Right now is the best time in all of history to be a kid!

35. **B.** The first known writing only appeared about 6,000 years ago. That means 97 percent of our history was never recorded.

# ACK EXAM 8

# Fun & Games

## Do You Really Know How to Play?

**1** Play-Doh smells yummy enough to eat! So why does it taste so bad?

- **A.** I don't think it bathes regularly.
- **B.** The Doh stands for its ingredients—dung, onions, and hairballs. Ew!
- **C.** It's made to taste bad on purpose.
- **D.** It's 100 percent factory made: nothing natural or edible involved!

**2** Which of these is a real job for grown-ups?

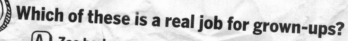

- **A.** Zoo barber
- **B.** Lego master builder
- **C.** Ping-Pong ball stomper
- **D.** "Whoosh!" sound artist for TV and movies.

Answers on page 137

### 3. What city was the original game of Monopoly based on?

**A.** Monopolea, a city that once existed in ancient Persia

**B.** Atlantic City, New Jersey

**C.** Las Vegas, Nevada

**D.** Emerald City. Ever notice the street names when watching *The Wizard of Oz*?

### 4. What is the length of time of the world's longest measured echo?

**A.** My own record is 7 seconds and I'm pretty good at shouting off mountaintops, so the world record can't be more than 10 seconds.

**B.** 23 seconds

**C.** 75 seconds

**D.** My mom says that when she saw Aerosmith in 1989 the sound echoed in her head for at least two days.

### 5. Who was the first superhero to gain superpowers from an accident during an experiment?

**A.** Spiderman

**B.** The Hulk

**C.** The Flash

**D.** In real life? My science teacher. When my baking-soda volcano went crazy, his voice rose so high it broke a window.

**6** What do first-place finishers win in the sport of wife carrying?

**A.** I just asked my mom and she says she's the one who carries my dad.

**B.** Glory, and the wife's weight in beer

**C.** $10,000 and a trophy

**D.** I don't know, but if this is on ESPN, I want to watch it.

**7** What is chessboxing?

**A.** Exactly what it sounds like: a brains and brawn competition.

**B.** A computer game, like in *Harry Potter*, in which the winning pieces pick up the losers and crush them.

**C.** A term used to describe smart boxers who find their opponents' flaws.

**D.** It's what happens when my two uncles play each other in chess. They take it waaaay too seriously.

**8** Which of these sports got canceled because of too many injuries?

**A.** Chessboxing. That's just a crazy idea anyway.

**B.** Cheese rolling

**C.** Dodgeball. Those balls really hurt!

**D.** Wife carrying

Answers on page 139

## 9 In a deck of cards, what are the King, Queen, and Jack known as?

**A.** Ummmmmm, the King, Queen, and Jack.

**B.** Trump cards

**C.** It depends. When my dad's friends are playing poker, they call them some pretty bad names if they lose.

**D.** The Court

## 10 In Egypt, game boards have been found in royal burial chambers dating back thousands of years. Can you guess what mysterious and ancient game the Pharaohs played?

**A.** The Word Pyramid

**B.** Checkers

**C.** Chess

**D.** Tomb Raider

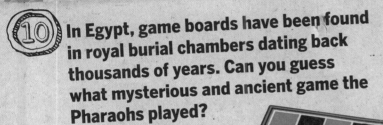

## 11 Where was the game of Chinese checkers invented?

**A.** I'm going to take a giant leap here and say China.

**B.** Germany

**C.** Egypt. They invented it after they got bored with the original checkers.

**D.** Mattel headquarters in California

# Answers
### From pages 134–135

1. **C.** Play-Doh's nice smell comes from added fragrances. But the company that makes it doesn't want you to eat it, even though it's not toxic. Play-Doh contains lots of salt, which tastes yucky in large amounts. It also contains borax, which is like laundry soap.

2. **B.** The folks at Lego carefully select 40 people to work around the world as master builders. They build all kinds of super-cool sculptures, buildings, and models out of the click-and-lock blocks.

3. **B.** All the names and places in the core Monopoly edition are based on ones that existed in Atlantic City when the game's owner, Parker Brothers, began selling it in 1935.

4. **C.** In 2014, a man from England climbed into a giant oil tank and used a recorded sound of a shotgun to make a 75-second echo!

5. **C.** The Flash, who first appeared in comics in 1940, got his super speed after a lab accident where he inhaled "hard water" vapors. No one really knows what those vapors were.

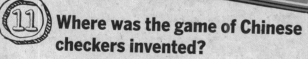

**12** Which video game has sold the most copies ever?

**A.** Minecraft. It's gotta be Minecraft. I love that game.

**B.** Grand Theft Auto V. People lined up outside stores overnight to buy the first copies.

**C.** Super Mario Bros. That game has been part of our family since my dad was a kid.

**D.** Tetris. An even more ancient game you threw in here to make this question appeal to my parents.

**13** How long was the world's longest hopscotch game?

**A.** Across a soccer field, around 360 feet

**B.** Down a runway at an airport, around 6,000 feet

**C.** 18,064 feet and 3 inches, measured precisely because it was done at a university

**D.** 19,800 feet, on the sidewalks of Detroit

**14** Which of these was once a popular sport in the Olympics?

**A.** Tug of war

**B.** Backwards running

**C.** Darts

**D.** Wife carrying

Answers on page 141

**15** The word 'muzjiks' has a particularly valuable use. What is it?

**A.** It can make the kids in my class think I'm insulting them in another language. Yo, muzjiks!

**B.** It can win me an awesome game of Scrabble.

**C.** It's the most commonly misspelled word in spelling bees.

**D.** It's the secret word to tell the pizza guy on the phone to get you free extra cheese.

**16** What should you be doing on International TableTop Day?

**A.** Playing a board game

**B.** It sounds like something involving a buffet, so I should be trying not to overeat.

**C.** Polishing all your tables until they glisten

**D.** Creating a table display of all your most prized possessions for friends and family

# Answers
## From pages 136-137

**6.** **B.** The Wife Carrying World Championships are held each year in Finland. Men carry a female teammate and race through an obstacle course. The glory of the win is the most important prize, but the winners also get the woman's weight in beer.

**7.** **A.** Chessboxers play 11 rounds: six of chess, and five of boxing. You can win either by knockout during a boxing round, or by checkmate during a chess round.

**8.** **B.** Cheese rolling started 200 years ago in England with competitors racing down a steep hill after a 9-pound round of cheese that could reach 70 miles per hour. Because the speeding cheese hurt so many spectators and runners, the official race was canceled in 2010. It continues on today, but not in any official way.

**9.** **C.** The names and images on playing cards have changed many times over the centuries. The Court cards of the King, Queen, and Jack, which represent royalty, are just the most recent changes. Many people call them "face cards," too.

**10.** **B.** Checkerboards were found in several tombs, including the one of Queen Hatasu.

**11.** **B.** Invented in Germany in 1892, Chinese checkers was actually based on an even older American game. Neither of them had any connection to China until the later game was introduced in China by the Japanese!

**17** What's it called when two jump ropes are whirled in opposite directions so you have to time it just right to jump over both of them?

A. Double Dutch

B. Trouble Touch

C. Toes-y Crunch

D. Lose Your Lunch

**18** Which of these is a real Crayola crayon color?

A. Fuzzy Wuzzy Brown

B. Granny Smith Apple Fungus

C. Schnauzer Lips Red

D. Mountain Gravel Beige

**19** What were monkey bars originally called?

A. The hang-around

B. Jungle gym

C. Orangutan bars

D. The climbing chamber of doom

Answers on page 143

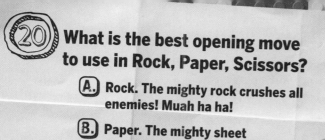

## 20. What is the best opening move to use in Rock, Paper, Scissors?

**A.** Rock. The mighty rock crushes all enemies! Muah ha ha!

**B.** Paper. The mighty sheet demolishes all crushers! Nyuck-nyuck!

**C.** Scissors. The mighty slicer savages all coverers! Yo ho ho!

**D.** I don't believe in confrontation so I just make a peace sign instead.

## 21. What was the soft NERF material used for before NERF guns became the most awesome indoor battle weapons ever?

**A.** It was made into long tubes for band teachers, who bonked kids when they hit sour notes.

**B.** It was used to help move race cars.

**C.** It was used as packing material for delicate electronic equipment.

**D.** It filled those cushioned toilet seats your grandma uses.

# Answers
## From pages 138-139

12. **C.** Introduced in 1984, the shape-tumbling game of Tetris has sold more than 143 million copies, way more than any other video game.

13. **C.** The game was played at the University of Guelph in Ontario, Canada, in 2011. But the world's longest hopscotch course was created a year later, in Detroit: 3.75 miles long, or 19,800 feet!

14. **A.** Tug of war lasted as an Olympic event from 1900-1920. Only two countries were winners of gold during that time: Great Britain had five gold medals and the United States had three.

15. **B.** Muzjiks, which is the name of some Russian peasants, gives you the highest possible score on an opening play in Scrabble. Play it on the right squares and you get a rock-socking 128 points!

16. **A.** International TableTop Day was created to bring friends and families together around a table with a game—board games, role playing games, card games, any kind you like. It takes place on a Saturday in late March or early April each year.

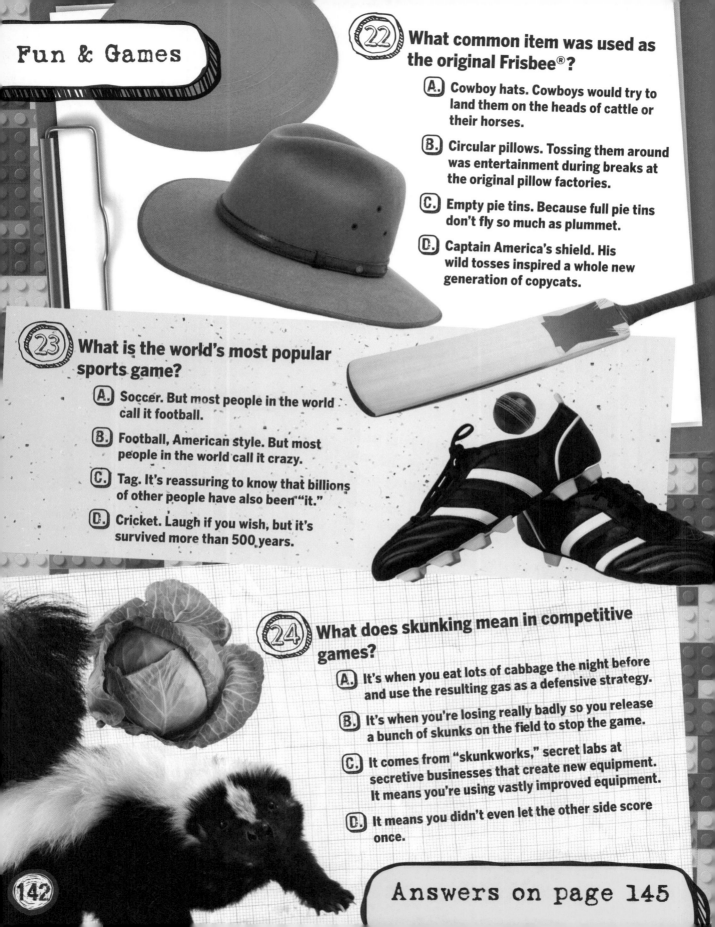

# Fun & Games

**22** What common item was used as the original Frisbee®?

**A.** Cowboy hats. Cowboys would try to land them on the heads of cattle or their horses.

**B.** Circular pillows. Tossing them around was entertainment during breaks at the original pillow factories.

**C.** Empty pie tins. Because full pie tins don't fly so much as plummet.

**D.** Captain America's shield. His wild tosses inspired a whole new generation of copycats.

**23** What is the world's most popular sports game?

**A.** Soccer. But most people in the world call it football.

**B.** Football, American style. But most people in the world call it crazy.

**C.** Tag. It's reassuring to know that billions of other people have also been "it."

**D.** Cricket. Laugh if you wish, but it's survived more than 500 years.

**24** What does skunking mean in competitive games?

**A.** It's when you eat lots of cabbage the night before and use the resulting gas as a defensive strategy.

**B.** It's when you're losing really badly so you release a bunch of skunks on the field to stop the game.

**C.** It comes from "skunkworks," secret labs at secretive businesses that create new equipment. It means you're using vastly improved equipment.

**D.** It means you didn't even let the other side score once.

Answers on page 145

## 25. A group of scientists ranked sports by the degree of difficulty and skill required. Which one was the hardest?

**A.** Downhill skiing. At night. In a forest. Chased by bears. Being chased by an avalanche.

**B.** Bathing cats

**C.** Boxing. It takes a college degree to hit someone properly.

**D.** Basketball. It uses every single muscle in your body, often all going in different directions.

## 26. In the same ranking, which sport had the lowest degree of difficulty?

**A.** Tiddlywinks. The ultimate game for action, excitement, and daredevil skill. If you're a frog.

**B.** Fishing. Also known as "excuse for napping."

**C.** Wife carrying. Assuming the wife is a willing participant.

**D.** Archery. You get a few blisters on your fingers but that's not so bad.

# Answers
## From pages 140-141

**17. A.** Double Dutch has been played in schoolyards for centuries. It was probably invented by rope makers who had to leap over long lengths of rope being spun together.

**18. A.** Crayola has 120 "core" crayon colors, including Fuzzy Wuzzy Brown. Colors also get retired from time to time, such as Raw Umber, Mulberry, Maize, and Blizzard Blue. In total, Crayola has introduced more than 400 colors since 1903.

**19. B.** When he invented it in 1920, lawyer Sebastian Hinton named it the jungle gym. It took another 35 years for the name monkey bars to catch on.

**20. B.** Experts say that most people tend to lead with rock. So start with paper, which covers rock, particularly when you're playing someone new whose patterns you don't know yet.

**21. B.** In the 1960s, drag racing cars had to be pushed to the starting line by trucks. The drivers who pushed the drag racers put foam-covered bars, called Nerf bars, on the front of their trucks to avoid damaging the race cars.

# Fun & Games

**27** What are these called?

A. Asterixes

B. Ninja throwing stars

C. Knucklebones

D. Dangerous to leave lying around, that's what they're called

321

**28** How long is a marathon?

A. 100 miles. An incredibly, amazingly painful 100 miles.

B. 26 miles and 385 yards. Though those are the longest 385 yards on all of Earth.

C. 24 miles

D. Almost 10 hours. That's how long it takes to watch a *Lord of the Rings* or *Star Wars* three-movie marathon.

**29** How many different positions of the squares are possible on a Rubik's Cube?

A. 21,626,000,637,244,928,000. That's easy, I figured it out in my head.

B. 21,626,001,637,244,928,000. Sorry, I completely forgot those one trillion other options.

C. 43,252,003,274,489,856,000. Sorry again, I forgot I needed to multiply by two!

D. Are you insane? There are 54 square locations. Six sides, nine squares a side. That's it.

Answers on page 147

**30 What's the best way to fill a water balloon?**

**A.** Right to the very top! I want maximum splash effect!

**B.** With fish sauce. Only problem, you lose all your friends when you do this.

**C.** Halfway full

**D.** About a quarter full

**31 What's the number-one rule of a pillow fight?**

**A.** Sneak attack. The element of surprise guarantees victory.

**B.** Yell, shriek, tickle, pounce; all's fair in pillow fights.

**C.** Stock up on ammo. Have a pillow in each hand, three more nearby for quick grabbing.

**D.** Use soft pillows only.

## Answers
### From pages 142-143

**22.** **C.** In the 1920s, university students "borrowed" used pie tins from their college cafeterias to throw around campus. The tins were made by the Frisbie Pie Company. In 1958, the Wham-O toy company ran with the idea and made the Frisbee we know and love today.

**23.** **A.** About 3.5 billion people take part in soccer around the world. Basketball is second, and cricket is a close third!

**24.** **D.** If you won and the other team didn't get even one point, they got skunked. The word comes from a Massachusetts term used first in the 1600s.

**25.** **C.** Experts note that boxing requires extreme levels of endurance, strength, power, speed, strategy, constant mental adjustments, and the ability to overcome fear.

**26.** **B.** Fishing has other advantages, namely getting to eat yummy fish, but it was by far the least demanding and difficult of the 60 sports ranked. It even finished behind billiards.

**32 Which of these burns the most calories?**

**A.** Hula-Hooping

**B.** Participating in a high-intensity hot dog eating contest

**C.** Bicycling

**D.** Avoiding doing your homework

# True or False

**1** A man in Vancouver, Canada, played Guitar Hero for 50 hours and 3 minutes without stopping.

◯ T  ◯ F

**2** The most expensive Xbox 360 game ever sold for $1,500.

◯ T  ◯ F

**3** The largest ever game of musical chairs was played with more than 8,000 people.

◯ T  ◯ F

**4** The game Yahtzee got its name from being invented on a boat.

◯ T  ◯ F

**5** The first game ever played by astronauts in space was I Spy.

◯ T  ◯ F

**6** Mario, the character from Super Mario Bros. was supposed to be Popeye.

◯ T  ◯ F

**7** Surgeons who play lots of video games perform better surgeries.

◯ T  ◯ F

**8** The original Mr. Potato Head came with three different kinds of potatoes.

◯ T  ◯ F

Answers on page 150

**9** The oldest known game item is the yo-yo.

○ T ○ F

**10** The original name for Scrabble was Scribble.

○ T ○ F

**11** When you commit a penalty serious enough to get thrown out of a soccer game, the referee holds up an orange card and makes you leave the field.

○ T ○ F

**12** Benjamin Franklin invented swimming fins.

○ T ○ F

**13** Lemon juice can be used as invisible ink.

○ T ○ F

**14** The largest game of dodgeball involved more than 6,000 people.

○ T ○ F

**15** The most popular recreational activity in the United States is bowling.

○ T ○ F

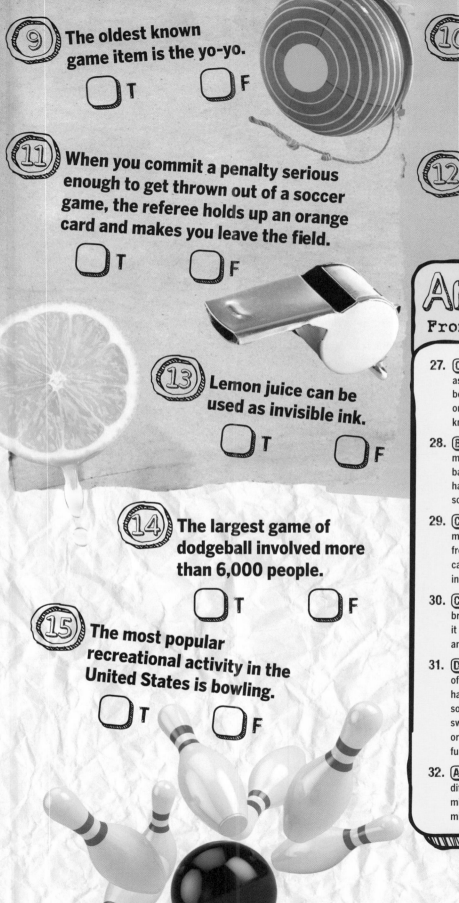

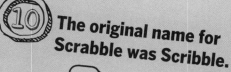

# Answers

From pages 144-145

27. **C.** This is a trick question. Today they're best known as jacks but the original name was knucklebones because they were made from sheep bones. Jacks is one of the oldest known games; in fact, no one really knows just how old it is.

28. **B.** The distance is based on the legend of a Greek messenger who ran 26 miles, 385 yards from the battle of Marathon to Athens to announce the Greeks had won. Sadly, the poor fellow collapsed and died as soon as he delivered the message.

29. **C.** What's even more staggering is that mathematicians have proven the puzzle can be solved from any starting position in 20 or less moves! A robot called Cubestormer 3 recently unscrambled the cube in just 3.253 seconds.

30. **C.** Halfway is perfect. Fill it more and it tends to break in your hand as you throw it. Too little water and it bounces off your target, who then picks it back up and pelts you with it!

31. **D.** Yeah, the boring but sensible answer. Organizers of the annual International Pillow Fight Day, which happens in dozens of cities around the world, list using soft pillows as rule number one. Other rules include swinging lightly, not swinging at people without pillows or with cameras, removing your glasses, focusing on fun, and not trying to hurt someone.

32. **A.** Hula-Hooping is swirly cool and it uses a ton of different muscle groups to burn more calories per minute of fun than most games—about 100 every 5-10 minutes.

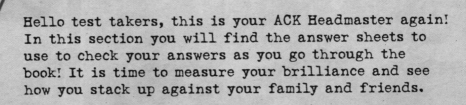

# True or False Answers

## Ack Exam 1: Geography

1. **FALSE:** Polar bears live in the Arctic, penguins live near the South Pole in the Antarctic.

2. **TRUE:** Think of the Equator as Earth's belt, running around its belly and keeping its pants up!

3. **FALSE:** A cartographer is someone who makes maps.

4. **TRUE:** Bit of a head fake, huh? It's called a sea because it's such a large lake.

5. **TRUE:** Turkey is one of six countries that span two continents.

6. **TRUE:** Just imagine the igloos you could make!

7. **FALSE:** Europe is the second smallest. Asia is the largest of Earth's seven continents.

8. **FALSE:** They call themselves Kiwis, not New Zealanders.

9. **TRUE:** It's been around since 301 A.D.

10. **TRUE:** The German cities of Hamburg and Frankfurt are the original homes of these classics.

11. **FALSE:** There's no such language as Swiss. People there speak German, French, Italian, and Romansh.

12. **FALSE:** Continental drift is the super-slow movement of the earth's giant landmasses.

## Ack Exam 2: Music

1. **TRUE:** Apparently, the tiny bugs enjoy music with a big, bad beat!

2. **TRUE:** These flies only live 14 days, but they're singing the whole time!

3. **FALSE:** But it's close—the small European country's military has about 250 members, while its orchestra has about 100 musicians.

4. **FALSE:** It actually takes 10 pianists more than 18 hours to play *Vexations* by composer Erik Satie.

5. **TRUE:** In fact, the fastest can rap more than 15 syllables per second.

6. **TRUE:** Bronze and silver trumpets were found in the grave of King Tut, an Egyptian pharaoh. Even older ones have been found in Central Asia.

7. **TRUE:** Well, sort of. A sperm whale blasts out a sound so loud it can stun a giant squid, an octopus, or any other tasty sea creatures it likes to eat.

8. **FALSE:** It was actually invented in Spain around the year 1500 A.D.

9. **TRUE:** More than 13,000 people showed up to do the hustle and the funky chicken dance.

10. **FALSE:** Many people think either Leo Fender or another man, Les Paul, made the first electric guitar, but it was actually invented by Adolph Rickenbacker. He began working on it in Los Angeles in the 1920s.

## Ack Exam 3: Human Body

1. **FALSE:** The nail on your middle finger grows fastest.

2. **FALSE:** The brain itself cannot feel pain, although the tissues around it can.

3. **TRUE:** Ker-pow! Your sneezes could pass a car on the highway!

4. **TRUE:** Many smaller bones fuse together as you get older.

5. **FALSE:** Your brain is a night owl. Why do you think you have all those crazy dreams?

6. **TRUE:** So turn that frown upside down, grumpy gills!

7. **TRUE:** Humans have exceptional night vision, especially when you consider we operate mostly in the daytime, unlike bats or owls.

8. **TRUE:** Even more if you eat baked beans or cabbage. Peee-yooo!

9. **FALSE:** Most people can do it. Only about 20-35 percent can't.

10. **TRUE:** Are you one? Then raise your hand! No, the other one!

11. **TRUE:** Can you imagine sleeping next to someone snoring like that?

12. **FALSE:** Actually, human eyes can see more than one million different color surfaces, from shiny silvers to neon reds to brilliant yellows.

## Ack Exam 4: Space

1. **FALSE.** It's only two-thirds the size.

2. **TRUE.** It's 43,440 miles wide!

3. **TRUE.** That's about one month.

4. **FALSE:** Only 12 astronauts have been there.

**5.** **TRUE.** Ouch, that's an instant sunburn.

**6.** **TRUE:** The Chinese Tiangong-1 and the International Space Station.

**7.** **TRUE:** But only 46 lbs. on the Moon!

**8.** **FALSE.** It burns blue-green. It just looks yellow from here.

**9.** **FALSE:** Only two—Phobos and Deimos.

**10.** **TRUE:** 8 minutes and 20 seconds to be exact.

**11.** **FALSE:** There is matter everywhere; it's just really spread out.

**12.** **FALSE:** It was a kind of beet soup called borscht.

**13.** **TRUE:** It was named after a mythical Chinese moon goddess.

**14.** **FALSE:** Stars come in more sizes than shoes. Ours is only medium sized.

**15.** **FALSE:** Their orbits are ellipses, a shape like an unstretched rubber band.

## Ack Exam 5: Art

**1.** **TRUE:** It was considered highly improper to show a woman's feet, so they were usually hidden under the hem of her dress.

**2.** **FALSE:** It is the Winter Palace and Hermitage in St. Petersburg, Russia. You'd have to walk 15 miles to see all three million works of art in its 322 galleries.

**3.** **TRUE:** The most common animal hairs were horse, ox, squirrel, and badger.

**4.** **TRUE:** But humans figured out how to make color pretty early on. The first evidence of man-made paint dates back roughly 100,000 years.

**5.** **FALSE:** Arushi Bhatnagar, from India, was only 11 months old in 2003 when she had an exhibition of her work and sold her first painting for about $100.

**6.** **TRUE:** But why did you have to tell me that? Now all I can think about is lemon squares topped with strawberries and orange sorbet.

**7.** **TRUE:** Almost as famous for his mustache as his art, Dali went on to become one of the most successful artists of the 20th century.

**8.** **FALSE:** They were first made around 500 A.D. in Central America but then popularized in the 1960s by hippies who wanted to look colorful and cool.

**9.** **FALSE:** Many paintings thousands of years old are exceptionally well preserved, but that's because of the extremely dry climate.

**10.** **FALSE:** This breaks down the bristles. Clean them well, then hang them to dry without letting them rest on the bristles.

**11.** **FALSE:** It's shocking, but experts estimate that only five percent is by women! Organizations are working hard today to raise the profile of women artists.

**12.** **TRUE:** His unique approach clearly worked; one of his abstract works sold for $140 million!

## Ack Exam 6: Nature

**1.** **TRUE:** Pretty scary, huh? Fortunately, they can only get about 12 feet high so you only have to climb 13 feet.

**2.** **TRUE:** People used to chew willow bark to relieve headaches until they learned how to make the medicinal compound in it.

**3.** **FALSE:** One common belief is that rain contains vitamin B12, but it doesn't.

**4.** **TRUE:** Water lilies in the Amazon rain forest easily get this big.

**5.** **FALSE:** Sharks don't have ANY bones. Their skeletons are made of cartilage—the same bendy stuff that gives your ears and nose their shape.

**6.** **TRUE:** It's really hard to digest grass and leaves, so giraffes need more than one stomach. Just ask a cow, which also has four.

**7.** **FALSE:** They live in many places outside Antarctica, including New Zealand, Australia, and South Africa.

**8.** **TRUE:** But they can still purr!

**9.** **TRUE:** They actually sound like lions! They can't purr, though.

**10.** **FALSE:** Their mouths are always closed under water, so they have to absorb it though their skin.

**11.** **TRUE:** Otherwise, the swallowing muscles in their long necks don't work properly.

**12.** **TRUE:** It does this to save energy and water during dry spells.

**13.** **FALSE:** But it has another cool claim to fame—it can move! It twitches for about five minutes each day.

**14.** **TRUE:** They pop above the surface and spit jets of water at nearby insects, almost always killing their prey on the first shot.

## Ack Exam 7: History

**1.** **FALSE:** But, in the late 1800s, a real plumber named Thomas Crapper improved toilets, making them very popular.

**2.** **TRUE:** Those doctors also had to pay any patients who got worse.

**3.** **FALSE:** Despite belief to the contrary, he was slightly above average height for that time.

**4.** **TRUE:** Most of the other signers didn't put ink to paper until August 2 of that year.

**5.** **TRUE:** In 1919, after the end of World War I, a Canadian soldier gave a bear cub that had been his brigade's mascot to the London zoo. The bear's name was Winnipeg, after the soldier's hometown. Author A. A. Milne's son, Christopher Robin, named his stuffed bear after the real bear and Milne used the name for his book.

**6.** **TRUE:** The Eternal Fire in Baba Gugur is fed by natural gas seeping through cracks in the rocks.

7. **TRUE:** Born in 356 B.C. in what is now Greece, Alexander was never defeated in a military battle.

8. **TRUE:** The fictional one was based on a real 80-ton whale that rammed boats and sank them in the early 1800s off the coast of South America.

9. **FALSE:** The ancient Egyptians hold this particular record. Their civilization lasted more than 4,000 years.

10. **FALSE:** It was actually the extremely tall mountains that surround most of China that kept it separate from much of the world.

11. **FALSE:** Hinduism, which originated in present-day India, dates back at least 6,000 years. There are more than one billion Hindus today, making it the third-largest religion, after Christianity and Islam.

12. **FALSE:** While slavery certainly existed in ancient Egypt, almost all the pyramid workers were paid for their labors.

## Ack Exam 8: Fun and Games

1. **TRUE:** In 2010, Zach Wong laid down a lick that lasted for more than two days.

2. **FALSE:** It was actually $3,000 for a super rare copy of the game Dead Space Ultra Limited Edition.

3. **TRUE:** 8,238 to be exact. It happened in Singapore in 1989.

4. **TRUE:** A Canadian couple came up with the game while sailing on their yacht.

5. **FALSE:** It was a game of chess played by Russian astronauts in 1970.

6. **TRUE:** Nintendo, the company that created Mario, couldn't get permission to use Popeye so they created Mario instead.

7. **TRUE:** A study showed that surgeons who were gamers made 37 percent fewer mistakes during surgery and worked 27 percent faster than non-gamer surgeons.

8. **FALSE:** He didn't even come with one! You only got legs, arms, eyes, and a mustache. You had to provide a real potato to stick them in.

9. **FALSE:** Dice are believed to be the oldest pieces of gaming equipment. They've been around since before recorded history.

10. **FALSE:** It was Lexiko, based on the word lexicon, which means vocabulary.

11. **FALSE:** He actually holds up a red card. Less serious penalties can get you a yellow card. If you get another yellow card in the same game, then you also get a red card and are thrown out.

12. **TRUE:** Franklin loved to swim so, at age 11, he invented fins to make him go faster. Unfortunately, they didn't work very well because he attached them to his hands.

13. **TRUE.** Dip a toothpick in it, write on a piece of paper and your words are invisible! To see them again, leave the paper in warm sunlight and the juice will turn brown.

14. **TRUE:** It was organized by the University of California and had 6,084 people picking each other off with a ball.

15. **TRUE:** More than 53 million Americans bowl every year.

## Answer Sheet Instructions

Rip out the answer sheets and either take the test, one subject at time, or for even more fun, hand them out to your family and friends. The last answer sheet has all the answers filled in, so be careful: If you tear it out, don't lose it! After you've filled out your sheet, line your sheet up against the filled-in version and hold it up to a light to see which ones you got wrong.

Don't feel bad if you've missed some! This is your chance to learn cool new facts, so to find out how you could have gotten some wrong, look up the detailed answers on the pages that follow the questions to find explanations. You'll be ready next time!

Good luck, test takers!

ACK Headmaster

# Answer Sheet

## Exam 1: Geography

1. (A) (B) (C) (D)
2. (A) (B) (C) (D)
3. (A) (B) (C) (D)
4. (A) (B) (C) (D)
5. (A) (B) (C) (D)
6. (A) (B) (C) (D)
7. (A) (B) (C) (D)
8. (A) (B) (C) (D)
9. (A) (B) (C) (D)
10. (A) (B) (C) (D)
11. (A) (B) (C) (D)
12. (A) (B) (C) (D)
13. (A) (B) (C) (D)
14. (A) (B) (C) (D)
15. (A) (B) (C) (D)
16. (A) (B) (C) (D)
17. (A) (B) (C) (D)
18. (A) (B) (C) (D)
19. (A) (B) (C) (D)
20. (A) (B) (C) (D)
21. (A) (B) (C) (D)
22. (A) (B) (C) (D)
23. (A) (B) (C) (D)
24. (A) (B) (C) (D)
25. (A) (B) (C) (D)
26. (A) (B) (C) (D)
27. (A) (B) (C) (D)
28. (A) (B) (C) (D)
29. (A) (B) (C) (D)
30. (A) (B) (C) (D)
31. (A) (B) (C) (D)
32. (A) (B) (C) (D)
33. (A) (B) (C) (D)
34. (A) (B) (C) (D)
35. (A) (B) (C) (D)
36. (A) (B) (C) (D)
37. (A) (B) (C) (D)
38. (A) (B) (C) (D)
39. (A) (B) (C) (D)
40. (A) (B) (C) (D)
41. (A) (B) (C) (D)
42. (A) (B) (C) (D)
43. (A) (B) (C) (D)
44. (A) (B) (C) (D)
45. (A) (B) (C) (D)
46. (A) (B) (C) (D)
47. (A) (B) (C) (D)
48. (A) (B) (C) (D)
49. (A) (B) (C) (D)
50. (A) (B) (C) (D)

## Exam 2: Music

1. (A) (B) (C) (D)
2. (A) (B) (C) (D)
3. (A) (B) (C) (D)
4. (A) (B) (C) (D)
5. (A) (B) (C) (D)
6. (A) (B) (C) (D)
7. (A) (B) (C) (D)
8. (A) (B) (C) (D)
9. (A) (B) (C) (D)
10. (A) (B) (C) (D)
11. (A) (B) (C) (D)
12. (A) (B) (C) (D)
13. (A) (B) (C) (D)
14. (A) (B) (C) (D)
15. (A) (B) (C) (D)
16. (A) (B) (C) (D)
17. (A) (B) (C) (D)
18. (A) (B) (C) (D)
19. (A) (B) (C) (D)
20. (A) (B) (C) (D)
21. (A) (B) (C) (D)
22. (A) (B) (C) (D)
23. (A) (B) (C) (D)
24. (A) (B) (C) (D)
25. (A) (B) (C) (D)
26. (A) (B) (C) (D)
27. (A) (B) (C) (D)
28. (A) (B) (C) (D)
29. (A) (B) (C) (D)
30. (A) (B) (C) (D)
31. (A) (B) (C) (D)
32. (A) (B) (C) (D)
33. (A) (B) (C) (D)
34. (A) (B) (C) (D)
35. (A) (B) (C) (D)
36. (A) (B) (C) (D)
37. (A) (B) (C) (D)
38. (A) (B) (C) (D)

## Exam 3: Human

1. (A) (B) (C) (D)
2. (A) (B) (C) (D)
3. (A) (B) (C) (D)
4. (A) (B) (C) (D)
5. (A) (B) (C) (D)
6. (A) (B) (C) (D)
7. (A) (B) (C) (D)
8. (A) (B) (C) (D)
9. (A) (B) (C) (D)
10. (A) (B) (C) (D)
11. (A) (B) (C) (D)
12. (A) (B) (C) (D)
13. (A) (B) (C) (D)
14. (A) (B) (C) (D)
15. (A) (B) (C) (D)
16. (A) (B) (C) (D)
17. (A) (B) (C) (D)
18. (A) (B) (C) (D)
19. (A) (B) (C) (D)
20. (A) (B) (C) (D)
21. (A) (B) (C) (D)
22. (A) (B) (C) (D)
23. (A) (B) (C) (D)
24. (A) (B) (C) (D)
25. (A) (B) (C) (D)
26. (A) (B) (C) (D)
27. (A) (B) (C) (D)

## Exam 4: Space

1. (A) (B) (C) (D)
2. (A) (B) (C) (D)
3. (A) (B) (C) (D)
4. (A) (B) (C) (D)
5. (A) (B) (C) (D)
6. (A) (B) (C) (D)
7. (A) (B) (C) (D)
8. (A) (B) (C) (D)
9. (A) (B) (C) (D)
10. (A) (B) (C) (D)
11. (A) (B) (C) (D)
12. (A) (B) (C) (D)
13. (A) (B) (C) (D)
14. (A) (B) (C) (D)
15. (A) (B) (C) (D)
16. (A) (B) (C) (D)
17. (A) (B) (C) (D)
18. (A) (B) (C) (D)
19. (A) (B) (C) (D)
20. (A) (B) (C) (D)
21. (A) (B) (C) (D)
22. (A) (B) (C) (D)
23. (A) (B) (C) (D)
24. (A) (B) (C) (D)
25. (A) (B) (C) (D)
26. (A) (B) (C) (D)
27. (A) (B) (C) (D)
28. (A) (B) (C) (D)
29. (A) (B) (C) (D)
30. (A) (B) (C) (D)
31. (A) (B) (C) (D)
32. (A) (B) (C) (D)
33. (A) (B) (C) (D)
34. (A) (B) (C) (D)
35. (A) (B) (C) (D)

## Exam 5: Art

1. (A) (B) (C) (D)
2. (A) (B) (C) (D)
3. (A) (B) (C) (D)
4. (A) (B) (C) (D)
5. (A) (B) (C) (D)
6. (A) (B) (C) (D)
7. (A) (B) (C) (D)
8. (A) (B) (C) (D)
9. (A) (B) (C) (D)
10. (A) (B) (C) (D)
11. (A) (B) (C) (D)
12. (A) (B) (C) (D)
13. (A) (B) (C) (D)
14. (A) (B) (C) (D)
15. (A) (B) (C) (D)
16. (A) (B) (C) (D)
17. (A) (B) (C) (D)
18. (A) (B) (C) (D)
19. (A) (B) (C) (D)
20. (A) (B) (C) (D)
21. (A) (B) (C) (D)
22. (A) (B) (C) (D)
23. (A) (B) (C) (D)
24. (A) (B) (C) (D)
25. (A) (B) (C) (D)
26. (A) (B) (C) (D)
27. (A) (B) (C) (D)
28. (A) (B) (C) (D)
29. (A) (B) (C) (D)
30. (A) (B) (C) (D)
31. (A) (B) (C) (D)
32. (A) (B) (C) (D)
33. (A) (B) (C) (D)
34. (A) (B) (C) (D)
35. (A) (B) (C) (D)

## Exam 6: Nature

1. (A) (B) (C) (D)
2. (A) (B) (C) (D)
3. (A) (B) (C) (D)
4. (A) (B) (C) (D)
5. (A) (B) (C) (D)
6. (A) (B) (C) (D)
7. (A) (B) (C) (D)
8. (A) (B) (C) (D)
9. (A) (B) (C) (D)
10. (A) (B) (C) (D)
11. (A) (B) (C) (D)
12. (A) (B) (C) (D)
13. (A) (B) (C) (D)
14. (A) (B) (C) (D)
15. (A) (B) (C) (D)
16. (A) (B) (C) (D)
17. (A) (B) (C) (D)
18. (A) (B) (C) (D)
19. (A) (B) (C) (D)
20. (A) (B) (C) (D)
21. (A) (B) (C) (D)
22. (A) (B) (C) (D)
23. (A) (B) (C) (D)
24. (A) (B) (C) (D)
25. (A) (B) (C) (D)
26. (A) (B) (C) (D)
27. (A) (B) (C) (D)
28. (A) (B) (C) (D)
29. (A) (B) (C) (D)
30. (A) (B) (C) (D)
31. (A) (B) (C) (D)
32. (A) (B) (C) (D)
33. (A) (B) (C) (D)
34. (A) (B) (C) (D)
35. (A) (B) (C) (D)

## Exam 7: History

1. (A) (B) (C) (D)
2. (A) (B) (C) (D)
3. (A) (B) (C) (D)
4. (A) (B) (C) (D)
5. (A) (B) (C) (D)
6. (A) (B) (C) (D)
7. (A) (B) (C) (D)
8. (A) (B) (C) (D)
9. (A) (B) (C) (D)
10. (A) (B) (C) (D)
11. (A) (B) (C) (D)
12. (A) (B) (C) (D)
13. (A) (B) (C) (D)
14. (A) (B) (C) (D)
15. (A) (B) (C) (D)
16. (A) (B) (C) (D)
17. (A) (B) (C) (D)
18. (A) (B) (C) (D)
19. (A) (B) (C) (D)
20. (A) (B) (C) (D)
21. (A) (B) (C) (D)
22. (A) (B) (C) (D)
23. (A) (B) (C) (D)
24. (A) (B) (C) (D)
25. (A) (B) (C) (D)
26. (A) (B) (C) (D)
27. (A) (B) (C) (D)
28. (A) (B) (C) (D)
29. (A) (B) (C) (D)
30. (A) (B) (C) (D)
31. (A) (B) (C) (D)
32. (A) (B) (C) (D)
33. (A) (B) (C) (D)
34. (A) (B) (C) (D)
35. (A) (B) (C) (D)

## Exam 8: Fun & Games

1. (A) (B) (C) (D)
2. (A) (B) (C) (D)
3. (A) (B) (C) (D)
4. (A) (B) (C) (D)
5. (A) (B) (C) (D)
6. (A) (B) (C) (D)
7. (A) (B) (C) (D)
8. (A) (B) (C) (D)
9. (A) (B) (C) (D)
10. (A) (B) (C) (D)
11. (A) (B) (C) (D)
12. (A) (B) (C) (D)
13. (A) (B) (C) (D)
14. (A) (B) (C) (D)
15. (A) (B) (C) (D)
16. (A) (B) (C) (D)
17. (A) (B) (C) (D)
18. (A) (B) (C) (D)
19. (A) (B) (C) (D)
20. (A) (B) (C) (D)
21. (A) (B) (C) (D)
22. (A) (B) (C) (D)
23. (A) (B) (C) (D)
24. (A) (B) (C) (D)
25. (A) (B) (C) (D)
26. (A) (B) (C) (D)
27. (A) (B) (C) (D)
28. (A) (B) (C) (D)
29. (A) (B) (C) (D)
30. (A) (B) (C) (D)
31. (A) (B) (C) (D)
32. (A) (B) (C) (D)

# Answer Sheet

## Exam 1: Geography

1. Ⓐ Ⓑ Ⓒ Ⓓ
2. Ⓐ Ⓑ Ⓒ Ⓓ
3. Ⓐ Ⓑ Ⓒ Ⓓ
4. Ⓐ Ⓑ Ⓒ Ⓓ
5. Ⓐ Ⓑ Ⓒ Ⓓ
6. Ⓐ Ⓑ Ⓒ Ⓓ
7. Ⓐ Ⓑ Ⓒ Ⓓ
8. Ⓐ Ⓑ Ⓒ Ⓓ
9. Ⓐ Ⓑ Ⓒ Ⓓ
10. Ⓐ Ⓑ Ⓒ Ⓓ
11. Ⓐ Ⓑ Ⓒ Ⓓ
12. Ⓐ Ⓑ Ⓒ Ⓓ
13. Ⓐ Ⓑ Ⓒ Ⓓ
14. Ⓐ Ⓑ Ⓒ Ⓓ
15. Ⓐ Ⓑ Ⓒ Ⓓ
16. Ⓐ Ⓑ Ⓒ Ⓓ
17. Ⓐ Ⓑ Ⓒ Ⓓ
18. Ⓐ Ⓑ Ⓒ Ⓓ
19. Ⓐ Ⓑ Ⓒ Ⓓ
20. Ⓐ Ⓑ Ⓒ Ⓓ
21. Ⓐ Ⓑ Ⓒ Ⓓ
22. Ⓐ Ⓑ Ⓒ Ⓓ
23. Ⓐ Ⓑ Ⓒ Ⓓ
24. Ⓐ Ⓑ Ⓒ Ⓓ
25. Ⓐ Ⓑ Ⓒ Ⓓ
26. Ⓐ Ⓑ Ⓒ Ⓓ
27. Ⓐ Ⓑ Ⓒ Ⓓ
28. Ⓐ Ⓑ Ⓒ Ⓓ
29. Ⓐ Ⓑ Ⓒ Ⓓ
30. Ⓐ Ⓑ Ⓒ Ⓓ
31. Ⓐ Ⓑ Ⓒ Ⓓ
32. Ⓐ Ⓑ Ⓒ Ⓓ
33. Ⓐ Ⓑ Ⓒ Ⓓ
34. Ⓐ Ⓑ Ⓒ Ⓓ
35. Ⓐ Ⓑ Ⓒ Ⓓ
36. Ⓐ Ⓑ Ⓒ Ⓓ
37. Ⓐ Ⓑ Ⓒ Ⓓ
38. Ⓐ Ⓑ Ⓒ Ⓓ
39. Ⓐ Ⓑ Ⓒ Ⓓ
40. Ⓐ Ⓑ Ⓒ Ⓓ
41. Ⓐ Ⓑ Ⓒ Ⓓ
42. Ⓐ Ⓑ Ⓒ Ⓓ
43. Ⓐ Ⓑ Ⓒ Ⓓ
44. Ⓐ Ⓑ Ⓒ Ⓓ
45. Ⓐ Ⓑ Ⓒ Ⓓ
46. Ⓐ Ⓑ Ⓒ Ⓓ
47. Ⓐ Ⓑ Ⓒ Ⓓ
48. Ⓐ Ⓑ Ⓒ Ⓓ
49. Ⓐ Ⓑ Ⓒ Ⓓ
50. Ⓐ Ⓑ Ⓒ Ⓓ

## Exam 2: Music

1. Ⓐ Ⓑ Ⓒ Ⓓ
2. Ⓐ Ⓑ Ⓒ Ⓓ
3. Ⓐ Ⓑ Ⓒ Ⓓ
4. Ⓐ Ⓑ Ⓒ Ⓓ
5. Ⓐ Ⓑ Ⓒ Ⓓ
6. Ⓐ Ⓑ Ⓒ Ⓓ
7. Ⓐ Ⓑ Ⓒ Ⓓ
8. Ⓐ Ⓑ Ⓒ Ⓓ
9. Ⓐ Ⓑ Ⓒ Ⓓ
10. Ⓐ Ⓑ Ⓒ Ⓓ
11. Ⓐ Ⓑ Ⓒ Ⓓ
12. Ⓐ Ⓑ Ⓒ Ⓓ
13. Ⓐ Ⓑ Ⓒ Ⓓ
14. Ⓐ Ⓑ Ⓒ Ⓓ
15. Ⓐ Ⓑ Ⓒ Ⓓ
16. Ⓐ Ⓑ Ⓒ Ⓓ
17. Ⓐ Ⓑ Ⓒ Ⓓ
18. Ⓐ Ⓑ Ⓒ Ⓓ
19. Ⓐ Ⓑ Ⓒ Ⓓ
20. Ⓐ Ⓑ Ⓒ Ⓓ
21. Ⓐ Ⓑ Ⓒ Ⓓ
22. Ⓐ Ⓑ Ⓒ Ⓓ
23. Ⓐ Ⓑ Ⓒ Ⓓ
24. Ⓐ Ⓑ Ⓒ Ⓓ
25. Ⓐ Ⓑ Ⓒ Ⓓ
26. Ⓐ Ⓑ Ⓒ Ⓓ
27. Ⓐ Ⓑ Ⓒ Ⓓ
28. Ⓐ Ⓑ Ⓒ Ⓓ
29. Ⓐ Ⓑ Ⓒ Ⓓ
30. Ⓐ Ⓑ Ⓒ Ⓓ
31. Ⓐ Ⓑ Ⓒ Ⓓ
32. Ⓐ Ⓑ Ⓒ Ⓓ
33. Ⓐ Ⓑ Ⓒ Ⓓ
34. Ⓐ Ⓑ Ⓒ Ⓓ
35. Ⓐ Ⓑ Ⓒ Ⓓ
36. Ⓐ Ⓑ Ⓒ Ⓓ
37. Ⓐ Ⓑ Ⓒ Ⓓ
38. Ⓐ Ⓑ Ⓒ Ⓓ

## Exam 3: Human

1. Ⓐ Ⓑ Ⓒ Ⓓ
2. Ⓐ Ⓑ Ⓒ Ⓓ
3. Ⓐ Ⓑ Ⓒ Ⓓ
4. Ⓐ Ⓑ Ⓒ Ⓓ
5. Ⓐ Ⓑ Ⓒ Ⓓ
6. Ⓐ Ⓑ Ⓒ Ⓓ
7. Ⓐ Ⓑ Ⓒ Ⓓ
8. Ⓐ Ⓑ Ⓒ Ⓓ
9. Ⓐ Ⓑ Ⓒ Ⓓ
10. Ⓐ Ⓑ Ⓒ Ⓓ
11. Ⓐ Ⓑ Ⓒ Ⓓ
12. Ⓐ Ⓑ Ⓒ Ⓓ
13. Ⓐ Ⓑ Ⓒ Ⓓ
14. Ⓐ Ⓑ Ⓒ Ⓓ
15. Ⓐ Ⓑ Ⓒ Ⓓ
16. Ⓐ Ⓑ Ⓒ Ⓓ
17. Ⓐ Ⓑ Ⓒ Ⓓ
18. Ⓐ Ⓑ Ⓒ Ⓓ
19. Ⓐ Ⓑ Ⓒ Ⓓ
20. Ⓐ Ⓑ Ⓒ Ⓓ
21. Ⓐ Ⓑ Ⓒ Ⓓ
22. Ⓐ Ⓑ Ⓒ Ⓓ
23. Ⓐ Ⓑ Ⓒ Ⓓ
24. Ⓐ Ⓑ Ⓒ Ⓓ
25. Ⓐ Ⓑ Ⓒ Ⓓ
26. Ⓐ Ⓑ Ⓒ Ⓓ
27. Ⓐ Ⓑ Ⓒ Ⓓ

## Exam 4: Space

1. Ⓐ Ⓑ Ⓒ Ⓓ
2. Ⓐ Ⓑ Ⓒ Ⓓ
3. Ⓐ Ⓑ Ⓒ Ⓓ
4. Ⓐ Ⓑ Ⓒ Ⓓ
5. Ⓐ Ⓑ Ⓒ Ⓓ
6. Ⓐ Ⓑ Ⓒ Ⓓ
7. Ⓐ Ⓑ Ⓒ Ⓓ
8. Ⓐ Ⓑ Ⓒ Ⓓ
9. Ⓐ Ⓑ Ⓒ Ⓓ
10. Ⓐ Ⓑ Ⓒ Ⓓ
11. Ⓐ Ⓑ Ⓒ Ⓓ
12. Ⓐ Ⓑ Ⓒ Ⓓ
13. Ⓐ Ⓑ Ⓒ Ⓓ
14. Ⓐ Ⓑ Ⓒ Ⓓ
15. Ⓐ Ⓑ Ⓒ Ⓓ
16. Ⓐ Ⓑ Ⓒ Ⓓ
17. Ⓐ Ⓑ Ⓒ Ⓓ
18. Ⓐ Ⓑ Ⓒ Ⓓ
19. Ⓐ Ⓑ Ⓒ Ⓓ
20. Ⓐ Ⓑ Ⓒ Ⓓ
21. Ⓐ Ⓑ Ⓒ Ⓓ
22. Ⓐ Ⓑ Ⓒ Ⓓ
23. Ⓐ Ⓑ Ⓒ Ⓓ
24. Ⓐ Ⓑ Ⓒ Ⓓ
25. Ⓐ Ⓑ Ⓒ Ⓓ
26. Ⓐ Ⓑ Ⓒ Ⓓ
27. Ⓐ Ⓑ Ⓒ Ⓓ
28. Ⓐ Ⓑ Ⓒ Ⓓ
29. Ⓐ Ⓑ Ⓒ Ⓓ
30. Ⓐ Ⓑ Ⓒ Ⓓ
31. Ⓐ Ⓑ Ⓒ Ⓓ
32. Ⓐ Ⓑ Ⓒ Ⓓ
33. Ⓐ Ⓑ Ⓒ Ⓓ
34. Ⓐ Ⓑ Ⓒ Ⓓ
35. Ⓐ Ⓑ Ⓒ Ⓓ
36. Ⓐ Ⓑ Ⓒ Ⓓ
37. Ⓐ Ⓑ Ⓒ Ⓓ

## Exam 5: Art

1. Ⓐ Ⓑ Ⓒ Ⓓ
2. Ⓐ Ⓑ Ⓒ Ⓓ
3. Ⓐ Ⓑ Ⓒ Ⓓ
4. Ⓐ Ⓑ Ⓒ Ⓓ
5. Ⓐ Ⓑ Ⓒ Ⓓ
6. Ⓐ Ⓑ Ⓒ Ⓓ
7. Ⓐ Ⓑ Ⓒ Ⓓ
8. Ⓐ Ⓑ Ⓒ Ⓓ
9. Ⓐ Ⓑ Ⓒ Ⓓ
10. Ⓐ Ⓑ Ⓒ Ⓓ
11. Ⓐ Ⓑ Ⓒ Ⓓ
12. Ⓐ Ⓑ Ⓒ Ⓓ
13. Ⓐ Ⓑ Ⓒ Ⓓ
14. Ⓐ Ⓑ Ⓒ Ⓓ
15. Ⓐ Ⓑ Ⓒ Ⓓ
16. Ⓐ Ⓑ Ⓒ Ⓓ
17. Ⓐ Ⓑ Ⓒ Ⓓ
18. Ⓐ Ⓑ Ⓒ Ⓓ
19. Ⓐ Ⓑ Ⓒ Ⓓ
20. Ⓐ Ⓑ Ⓒ Ⓓ
21. Ⓐ Ⓑ Ⓒ Ⓓ
22. Ⓐ Ⓑ Ⓒ Ⓓ
23. Ⓐ Ⓑ Ⓒ Ⓓ
24. Ⓐ Ⓑ Ⓒ Ⓓ
25. Ⓐ Ⓑ Ⓒ Ⓓ
26. Ⓐ Ⓑ Ⓒ Ⓓ
27. Ⓐ Ⓑ Ⓒ Ⓓ
28. Ⓐ Ⓑ Ⓒ Ⓓ
29. Ⓐ Ⓑ Ⓒ Ⓓ
30. Ⓐ Ⓑ Ⓒ Ⓓ
31. Ⓐ Ⓑ Ⓒ Ⓓ
32. Ⓐ Ⓑ Ⓒ Ⓓ
33. Ⓐ Ⓑ Ⓒ Ⓓ
34. Ⓐ Ⓑ Ⓒ Ⓓ
35. Ⓐ Ⓑ Ⓒ Ⓓ

## Exam 6: Nature

1. Ⓐ Ⓑ Ⓒ Ⓓ
2. Ⓐ Ⓑ Ⓒ Ⓓ

## Exam 7: History

1. Ⓐ Ⓑ Ⓒ Ⓓ
2. Ⓐ Ⓑ Ⓒ Ⓓ
3. Ⓐ Ⓑ Ⓒ Ⓓ
4. Ⓐ Ⓑ Ⓒ Ⓓ
5. Ⓐ Ⓑ Ⓒ Ⓓ
6. Ⓐ Ⓑ Ⓒ Ⓓ
7. Ⓐ Ⓑ Ⓒ Ⓓ
8. Ⓐ Ⓑ Ⓒ Ⓓ
9. Ⓐ Ⓑ Ⓒ Ⓓ
10. Ⓐ Ⓑ Ⓒ Ⓓ
11. Ⓐ Ⓑ Ⓒ Ⓓ
12. Ⓐ Ⓑ Ⓒ Ⓓ
13. Ⓐ Ⓑ Ⓒ Ⓓ
14. Ⓐ Ⓑ Ⓒ Ⓓ
15. Ⓐ Ⓑ Ⓒ Ⓓ
16. Ⓐ Ⓑ Ⓒ Ⓓ
17. Ⓐ Ⓑ Ⓒ Ⓓ
18. Ⓐ Ⓑ Ⓒ Ⓓ
19. Ⓐ Ⓑ Ⓒ Ⓓ
20. Ⓐ Ⓑ Ⓒ Ⓓ
21. Ⓐ Ⓑ Ⓒ Ⓓ
22. Ⓐ Ⓑ Ⓒ Ⓓ
23. Ⓐ Ⓑ Ⓒ Ⓓ
24. Ⓐ Ⓑ Ⓒ Ⓓ
25. Ⓐ Ⓑ Ⓒ Ⓓ
26. Ⓐ Ⓑ Ⓒ Ⓓ
27. Ⓐ Ⓑ Ⓒ Ⓓ
28. Ⓐ Ⓑ Ⓒ Ⓓ
29. Ⓐ Ⓑ Ⓒ Ⓓ
30. Ⓐ Ⓑ Ⓒ Ⓓ
31. Ⓐ Ⓑ Ⓒ Ⓓ
32. Ⓐ Ⓑ Ⓒ Ⓓ
33. Ⓐ Ⓑ Ⓒ Ⓓ
34. Ⓐ Ⓑ Ⓒ Ⓓ
35. Ⓐ Ⓑ Ⓒ Ⓓ

## Exam 8: Fun & Games

1. Ⓐ Ⓑ Ⓒ Ⓓ
2. Ⓐ Ⓑ Ⓒ Ⓓ
3. Ⓐ Ⓑ Ⓒ Ⓓ
4. Ⓐ Ⓑ Ⓒ Ⓓ
5. Ⓐ Ⓑ Ⓒ Ⓓ
6. Ⓐ Ⓑ Ⓒ Ⓓ
7. Ⓐ Ⓑ Ⓒ Ⓓ
8. Ⓐ Ⓑ Ⓒ Ⓓ
9. Ⓐ Ⓑ Ⓒ Ⓓ
10. Ⓐ Ⓑ Ⓒ Ⓓ
11. Ⓐ Ⓑ Ⓒ Ⓓ
12. Ⓐ Ⓑ Ⓒ Ⓓ
13. Ⓐ Ⓑ Ⓒ Ⓓ
14. Ⓐ Ⓑ Ⓒ Ⓓ
15. Ⓐ Ⓑ Ⓒ Ⓓ
16. Ⓐ Ⓑ Ⓒ Ⓓ
17. Ⓐ Ⓑ Ⓒ Ⓓ
18. Ⓐ Ⓑ Ⓒ Ⓓ
19. Ⓐ Ⓑ Ⓒ Ⓓ
20. Ⓐ Ⓑ Ⓒ Ⓓ
21. Ⓐ Ⓑ Ⓒ Ⓓ
22. Ⓐ Ⓑ Ⓒ Ⓓ
23. Ⓐ Ⓑ Ⓒ Ⓓ
24. Ⓐ Ⓑ Ⓒ Ⓓ
25. Ⓐ Ⓑ Ⓒ Ⓓ
26. Ⓐ Ⓑ Ⓒ Ⓓ
27. Ⓐ Ⓑ Ⓒ Ⓓ
28. Ⓐ Ⓑ Ⓒ Ⓓ
29. Ⓐ Ⓑ Ⓒ Ⓓ
30. Ⓐ Ⓑ Ⓒ Ⓓ
31. Ⓐ Ⓑ Ⓒ Ⓓ
32. Ⓐ Ⓑ Ⓒ Ⓓ

# Answer Sheet

## Exam 1: Geography

1. Ⓐ Ⓑ Ⓒ Ⓓ
2. Ⓐ Ⓑ Ⓒ Ⓓ
3. Ⓐ Ⓑ Ⓒ Ⓓ
4. Ⓐ Ⓑ Ⓒ Ⓓ
5. Ⓐ Ⓑ Ⓒ Ⓓ
6. Ⓐ Ⓑ Ⓒ Ⓓ
7. Ⓐ Ⓑ Ⓒ Ⓓ
8. Ⓐ Ⓑ Ⓒ Ⓓ
9. Ⓐ Ⓑ Ⓒ Ⓓ
10. Ⓐ Ⓑ Ⓒ Ⓓ
11. Ⓐ Ⓑ Ⓒ Ⓓ
12. Ⓐ Ⓑ Ⓒ Ⓓ
13. Ⓐ Ⓑ Ⓒ Ⓓ
14. Ⓐ Ⓑ Ⓒ Ⓓ
15. Ⓐ Ⓑ Ⓒ Ⓓ
16. Ⓐ Ⓑ Ⓒ Ⓓ
17. Ⓐ Ⓑ Ⓒ Ⓓ
18. Ⓐ Ⓑ Ⓒ Ⓓ
19. Ⓐ Ⓑ Ⓒ Ⓓ
20. Ⓐ Ⓑ Ⓒ Ⓓ
21. Ⓐ Ⓑ Ⓒ Ⓓ
22. Ⓐ Ⓑ Ⓒ Ⓓ
23. Ⓐ Ⓑ Ⓒ Ⓓ
24. Ⓐ Ⓑ Ⓒ Ⓓ
25. Ⓐ Ⓑ Ⓒ Ⓓ
26. Ⓐ Ⓑ Ⓒ Ⓓ
27. Ⓐ Ⓑ Ⓒ Ⓓ
28. Ⓐ Ⓑ Ⓒ Ⓓ
29. Ⓐ Ⓑ Ⓒ Ⓓ
30. Ⓐ Ⓑ Ⓒ Ⓓ
31. Ⓐ Ⓑ Ⓒ Ⓓ
32. Ⓐ Ⓑ Ⓒ Ⓓ
33. Ⓐ Ⓑ Ⓒ Ⓓ
34. Ⓐ Ⓑ Ⓒ Ⓓ
35. Ⓐ Ⓑ Ⓒ Ⓓ
36. Ⓐ Ⓑ Ⓒ Ⓓ
37. Ⓐ Ⓑ Ⓒ Ⓓ
38. Ⓐ Ⓑ Ⓒ Ⓓ
39. Ⓐ Ⓑ Ⓒ Ⓓ
40. Ⓐ Ⓑ Ⓒ Ⓓ
41. Ⓐ Ⓑ Ⓒ Ⓓ
42. Ⓐ Ⓑ Ⓒ Ⓓ
43. Ⓐ Ⓑ Ⓒ Ⓓ
44. Ⓐ Ⓑ Ⓒ Ⓓ
45. Ⓐ Ⓑ Ⓒ Ⓓ
46. Ⓐ Ⓑ Ⓒ Ⓓ
47. Ⓐ Ⓑ Ⓒ Ⓓ
48. Ⓐ Ⓑ Ⓒ Ⓓ
49. Ⓐ Ⓑ Ⓒ Ⓓ
50. Ⓐ Ⓑ Ⓒ Ⓓ

## Exam 2: Music

1. Ⓐ Ⓑ Ⓒ Ⓓ
2. Ⓐ Ⓑ Ⓒ Ⓓ
3. Ⓐ Ⓑ Ⓒ Ⓓ
4. Ⓐ Ⓑ Ⓒ Ⓓ
5. Ⓐ Ⓑ Ⓒ Ⓓ
6. Ⓐ Ⓑ Ⓒ Ⓓ
7. Ⓐ Ⓑ Ⓒ Ⓓ
8. Ⓐ Ⓑ Ⓒ Ⓓ
9. Ⓐ Ⓑ Ⓒ Ⓓ
10. Ⓐ Ⓑ Ⓒ Ⓓ
11. Ⓐ Ⓑ Ⓒ Ⓓ
12. Ⓐ Ⓑ Ⓒ Ⓓ
13. Ⓐ Ⓑ Ⓒ Ⓓ
14. Ⓐ Ⓑ Ⓒ Ⓓ
15. Ⓐ Ⓑ Ⓒ Ⓓ
16. Ⓐ Ⓑ Ⓒ Ⓓ
17. Ⓐ Ⓑ Ⓒ Ⓓ
18. Ⓐ Ⓑ Ⓒ Ⓓ
19. Ⓐ Ⓑ Ⓒ Ⓓ
20. Ⓐ Ⓑ Ⓒ Ⓓ
21. Ⓐ Ⓑ Ⓒ Ⓓ
22. Ⓐ Ⓑ Ⓒ Ⓓ
23. Ⓐ Ⓑ Ⓒ Ⓓ
24. Ⓐ Ⓑ Ⓒ Ⓓ
25. Ⓐ Ⓑ Ⓒ Ⓓ
26. Ⓐ Ⓑ Ⓒ Ⓓ
27. Ⓐ Ⓑ Ⓒ Ⓓ
28. Ⓐ Ⓑ Ⓒ Ⓓ
29. Ⓐ Ⓑ Ⓒ Ⓓ
30. Ⓐ Ⓑ Ⓒ Ⓓ
31. Ⓐ Ⓑ Ⓒ Ⓓ
32. Ⓐ Ⓑ Ⓒ Ⓓ
33. Ⓐ Ⓑ Ⓒ Ⓓ
34. Ⓐ Ⓑ Ⓒ Ⓓ
35. Ⓐ Ⓑ Ⓒ Ⓓ
36. Ⓐ Ⓑ Ⓒ Ⓓ
37. Ⓐ Ⓑ Ⓒ Ⓓ
38. Ⓐ Ⓑ Ⓒ Ⓓ

## Exam 3: Human

1. Ⓐ Ⓑ Ⓒ Ⓓ
2. Ⓐ Ⓑ Ⓒ Ⓓ
3. Ⓐ Ⓑ Ⓒ Ⓓ
4. Ⓐ Ⓑ Ⓒ Ⓓ
5. Ⓐ Ⓑ Ⓒ Ⓓ
6. Ⓐ Ⓑ Ⓒ Ⓓ
7. Ⓐ Ⓑ Ⓒ Ⓓ
8. Ⓐ Ⓑ Ⓒ Ⓓ
9. Ⓐ Ⓑ Ⓒ Ⓓ
10. Ⓐ Ⓑ Ⓒ Ⓓ
11. Ⓐ Ⓑ Ⓒ Ⓓ
12. Ⓐ Ⓑ Ⓒ Ⓓ
13. Ⓐ Ⓑ Ⓒ Ⓓ
14. Ⓐ Ⓑ Ⓒ Ⓓ
15. Ⓐ Ⓑ Ⓒ Ⓓ
16. Ⓐ Ⓑ Ⓒ Ⓓ
17. Ⓐ Ⓑ Ⓒ Ⓓ
18. Ⓐ Ⓑ Ⓒ Ⓓ
19. Ⓐ Ⓑ Ⓒ Ⓓ
20. Ⓐ Ⓑ Ⓒ Ⓓ
21. Ⓐ Ⓑ Ⓒ Ⓓ
22. Ⓐ Ⓑ Ⓒ Ⓓ
23. Ⓐ Ⓑ Ⓒ Ⓓ
24. Ⓐ Ⓑ Ⓒ Ⓓ
25. Ⓐ Ⓑ Ⓒ Ⓓ
26. Ⓐ Ⓑ Ⓒ Ⓓ
27. Ⓐ Ⓑ Ⓒ Ⓓ
28. Ⓐ Ⓑ Ⓒ Ⓓ
29. Ⓐ Ⓑ Ⓒ Ⓓ
30. Ⓐ Ⓑ Ⓒ Ⓓ
31. Ⓐ Ⓑ Ⓒ Ⓓ
32. Ⓐ Ⓑ Ⓒ Ⓓ
33. Ⓐ Ⓑ Ⓒ Ⓓ
34. Ⓐ Ⓑ Ⓒ Ⓓ
35. Ⓐ Ⓑ Ⓒ Ⓓ
36. Ⓐ Ⓑ Ⓒ Ⓓ
37. Ⓐ Ⓑ Ⓒ Ⓓ

## Exam 4: Space

1. Ⓐ Ⓑ Ⓒ Ⓓ
2. Ⓐ Ⓑ Ⓒ Ⓓ
3. Ⓐ Ⓑ Ⓒ Ⓓ
4. Ⓐ Ⓑ Ⓒ Ⓓ
5. Ⓐ Ⓑ Ⓒ Ⓓ
6. Ⓐ Ⓑ Ⓒ Ⓓ
7. Ⓐ Ⓑ Ⓒ Ⓓ
8. Ⓐ Ⓑ Ⓒ Ⓓ
9. Ⓐ Ⓑ Ⓒ Ⓓ
10. Ⓐ Ⓑ Ⓒ Ⓓ
11. Ⓐ Ⓑ Ⓒ Ⓓ
12. Ⓐ Ⓑ Ⓒ Ⓓ
13. Ⓐ Ⓑ Ⓒ Ⓓ
14. Ⓐ Ⓑ Ⓒ Ⓓ
15. Ⓐ Ⓑ Ⓒ Ⓓ
16. Ⓐ Ⓑ Ⓒ Ⓓ
17. Ⓐ Ⓑ Ⓒ Ⓓ
18. Ⓐ Ⓑ Ⓒ Ⓓ
19. Ⓐ Ⓑ Ⓒ Ⓓ
20. Ⓐ Ⓑ Ⓒ Ⓓ
21. Ⓐ Ⓑ Ⓒ Ⓓ
22. Ⓐ Ⓑ Ⓒ Ⓓ
23. Ⓐ Ⓑ Ⓒ Ⓓ
24. Ⓐ Ⓑ Ⓒ Ⓓ
25. Ⓐ Ⓑ Ⓒ Ⓓ
26. Ⓐ Ⓑ Ⓒ Ⓓ
27. Ⓐ Ⓑ Ⓒ Ⓓ
28. Ⓐ Ⓑ Ⓒ Ⓓ
29. Ⓐ Ⓑ Ⓒ Ⓓ
30. Ⓐ Ⓑ Ⓒ Ⓓ
31. Ⓐ Ⓑ Ⓒ Ⓓ
32. Ⓐ Ⓑ Ⓒ Ⓓ
33. Ⓐ Ⓑ Ⓒ Ⓓ
34. Ⓐ Ⓑ Ⓒ Ⓓ
35. Ⓐ Ⓑ Ⓒ Ⓓ

## Exam 5: Art

1. Ⓐ Ⓑ Ⓒ Ⓓ
2. Ⓐ Ⓑ Ⓒ Ⓓ
3. Ⓐ Ⓑ Ⓒ Ⓓ
4. Ⓐ Ⓑ Ⓒ Ⓓ
5. Ⓐ Ⓑ Ⓒ Ⓓ
6. Ⓐ Ⓑ Ⓒ Ⓓ
7. Ⓐ Ⓑ Ⓒ Ⓓ
8. Ⓐ Ⓑ Ⓒ Ⓓ
9. Ⓐ Ⓑ Ⓒ Ⓓ
10. Ⓐ Ⓑ Ⓒ Ⓓ
11. Ⓐ Ⓑ Ⓒ Ⓓ
12. Ⓐ Ⓑ Ⓒ Ⓓ
13. Ⓐ Ⓑ Ⓒ Ⓓ
14. Ⓐ Ⓑ Ⓒ Ⓓ
15. Ⓐ Ⓑ Ⓒ Ⓓ
16. Ⓐ Ⓑ Ⓒ Ⓓ
17. Ⓐ Ⓑ Ⓒ Ⓓ
18. Ⓐ Ⓑ Ⓒ Ⓓ
19. Ⓐ Ⓑ Ⓒ Ⓓ
20. Ⓐ Ⓑ Ⓒ Ⓓ
21. Ⓐ Ⓑ Ⓒ Ⓓ
22. Ⓐ Ⓑ Ⓒ Ⓓ
23. Ⓐ Ⓑ Ⓒ Ⓓ
24. Ⓐ Ⓑ Ⓒ Ⓓ
25. Ⓐ Ⓑ Ⓒ Ⓓ
26. Ⓐ Ⓑ Ⓒ Ⓓ
27. Ⓐ Ⓑ Ⓒ Ⓓ
28. Ⓐ Ⓑ Ⓒ Ⓓ
29. Ⓐ Ⓑ Ⓒ Ⓓ
30. Ⓐ Ⓑ Ⓒ Ⓓ
31. Ⓐ Ⓑ Ⓒ Ⓓ
32. Ⓐ Ⓑ Ⓒ Ⓓ
33. Ⓐ Ⓑ Ⓒ Ⓓ
34. Ⓐ Ⓑ Ⓒ Ⓓ
35. Ⓐ Ⓑ Ⓒ Ⓓ

## Exam 6: Nature

1. Ⓐ Ⓑ Ⓒ Ⓓ
2. Ⓐ Ⓑ Ⓒ Ⓓ

## Exam 7: History

1. Ⓐ Ⓑ Ⓒ Ⓓ
2. Ⓐ Ⓑ Ⓒ Ⓓ
3. Ⓐ Ⓑ Ⓒ Ⓓ
4. Ⓐ Ⓑ Ⓒ Ⓓ
5. Ⓐ Ⓑ Ⓒ Ⓓ
6. Ⓐ Ⓑ Ⓒ Ⓓ
7. Ⓐ Ⓑ Ⓒ Ⓓ
8. Ⓐ Ⓑ Ⓒ Ⓓ
9. Ⓐ Ⓑ Ⓒ Ⓓ
10. Ⓐ Ⓑ Ⓒ Ⓓ
11. Ⓐ Ⓑ Ⓒ Ⓓ
12. Ⓐ Ⓑ Ⓒ Ⓓ
13. Ⓐ Ⓑ Ⓒ Ⓓ
14. Ⓐ Ⓑ Ⓒ Ⓓ
15. Ⓐ Ⓑ Ⓒ Ⓓ
16. Ⓐ Ⓑ Ⓒ Ⓓ
17. Ⓐ Ⓑ Ⓒ Ⓓ
18. Ⓐ Ⓑ Ⓒ Ⓓ
19. Ⓐ Ⓑ Ⓒ Ⓓ
20. Ⓐ Ⓑ Ⓒ Ⓓ
21. Ⓐ Ⓑ Ⓒ Ⓓ
22. Ⓐ Ⓑ Ⓒ Ⓓ
23. Ⓐ Ⓑ Ⓒ Ⓓ
24. Ⓐ Ⓑ Ⓒ Ⓓ
25. Ⓐ Ⓑ Ⓒ Ⓓ
26. Ⓐ Ⓑ Ⓒ Ⓓ
27. Ⓐ Ⓑ Ⓒ Ⓓ
28. Ⓐ Ⓑ Ⓒ Ⓓ
29. Ⓐ Ⓑ Ⓒ Ⓓ
30. Ⓐ Ⓑ Ⓒ Ⓓ
31. Ⓐ Ⓑ Ⓒ Ⓓ
32. Ⓐ Ⓑ Ⓒ Ⓓ

## Exam 8: Fun & Games

1. Ⓐ Ⓑ Ⓒ Ⓓ
2. Ⓐ Ⓑ Ⓒ Ⓓ
3. Ⓐ Ⓑ Ⓒ Ⓓ
4. Ⓐ Ⓑ Ⓒ Ⓓ
5. Ⓐ Ⓑ Ⓒ Ⓓ
6. Ⓐ Ⓑ Ⓒ Ⓓ
7. Ⓐ Ⓑ Ⓒ Ⓓ
8. Ⓐ Ⓑ Ⓒ Ⓓ
9. Ⓐ Ⓑ Ⓒ Ⓓ
10. Ⓐ Ⓑ Ⓒ Ⓓ
11. Ⓐ Ⓑ Ⓒ Ⓓ
12. Ⓐ Ⓑ Ⓒ Ⓓ
13. Ⓐ Ⓑ Ⓒ Ⓓ
14. Ⓐ Ⓑ Ⓒ Ⓓ
15. Ⓐ Ⓑ Ⓒ Ⓓ
16. Ⓐ Ⓑ Ⓒ Ⓓ
17. Ⓐ Ⓑ Ⓒ Ⓓ
18. Ⓐ Ⓑ Ⓒ Ⓓ
19. Ⓐ Ⓑ Ⓒ Ⓓ
20. Ⓐ Ⓑ Ⓒ Ⓓ
21. Ⓐ Ⓑ Ⓒ Ⓓ
22. Ⓐ Ⓑ Ⓒ Ⓓ
23. Ⓐ Ⓑ Ⓒ Ⓓ
24. Ⓐ Ⓑ Ⓒ Ⓓ
25. Ⓐ Ⓑ Ⓒ Ⓓ
26. Ⓐ Ⓑ Ⓒ Ⓓ
27. Ⓐ Ⓑ Ⓒ Ⓓ
28. Ⓐ Ⓑ Ⓒ Ⓓ
29. Ⓐ Ⓑ Ⓒ Ⓓ
30. Ⓐ Ⓑ Ⓒ Ⓓ
31. Ⓐ Ⓑ Ⓒ Ⓓ
32. Ⓐ Ⓑ Ⓒ Ⓓ

# Answer Sheet

## Exam 1: Geography

1. A B C D
2. A B C D
3. A B C D
4. A B C D
5. A B C D
6. A B C D
7. A B C D
8. A B C D
9. A B C D
10. A B C D
11. A B C D
12. A B C D
13. A B C D
14. A B C D
15. A B C D
16. A B C D
17. A B C D
18. A B C D
19. A B C D
20. A B C D
21. A B C D
22. A B C D
23. A B C D
24. A B C D
25. A B C D
26. A B C D
27. A B C D
28. A B C D
29. A B C D
30. A B C D
31. A B C D
32. A B C D
33. A B C D
34. A B C D
35. A B C D
36. A B C D
37. A B C D
38. A B C D
39. A B C D
40. A B C D
41. A B C D
42. A B C D
43. A B C D
44. A B C D
45. A B C D
46. A B C D
47. A B C D
48. A B C D
49. A B C D
50. A B C D

## Exam 2: Music

1. A B C D
2. A B C D
3. A B C D
4. A B C D
5. A B C D
6. A B C D
7. A B C D
8. A B C D
9. A B C D
10. A B C D
11. A B C D
12. A B C D
13. A B C D
14. A B C D
15. A B C D
16. A B C D
17. A B C D
18. A B C D
19. A B C D
20. A B C D
21. A B C D
22. A B C D
23. A B C D
24. A B C D
25. A B C D
26. A B C D
27. A B C D
28. A B C D
29. A B C D
30. A B C D
31. A B C D
32. A B C D
33. A B C D
34. A B C D
35. A B C D
36. A B C D
37. A B C D
38. A B C D

## Exam 3: Human

1. A B C D
2. A B C D
3. A B C D
4. A B C D
5. A B C D
6. A B C D
7. A B C D
8. A B C D
9. A B C D
10. A B C D
11. A B C D
12. A B C D
13. A B C D
14. A B C D
15. A B C D
16. A B C D
17. A B C D
18. A B C D
19. A B C D
20. A B C D
21. A B C D
22. A B C D
23. A B C D
24. A B C D
25. A B C D
26. A B C D
27. A B C D
28. A B C D
29. A B C D
30. A B C D
31. A B C D
32. A B C D
33. A B C D
34. A B C D
35. A B C D
36. A B C D
37. A B C D

## Exam 4: Space

1. A B C D
2. A B C D
3. A B C D
4. A B C D
5. A B C D
6. A B C D
7. A B C D
8. A B C D
9. A B C D
10. A B C D
11. A B C D
12. A B C D
13. A B C D
14. A B C D
15. A B C D
16. A B C D
17. A B C D
18. A B C D
19. A B C D
20. A B C D
21. A B C D
22. A B C D
23. A B C D
24. A B C D
25. A B C D
26. A B C D
27. A B C D

## Exam 5: Art

1. A B C D
2. A B C D
3. A B C D
4. A B C D
5. A B C D
6. A B C D
7. A B C D
8. A B C D
9. A B C D
10. A B C D
11. A B C D
12. A B C D
13. A B C D
14. A B C D
15. A B C D
16. A B C D
17. A B C D
18. A B C D
19. A B C D
20. A B C D
21. A B C D
22. A B C D
23. A B C D
24. A B C D
25. A B C D
26. A B C D
27. A B C D
28. A B C D
29. A B C D
30. A B C D
31. A B C D
32. A B C D
33. A B C D
34. A B C D
35. A B C D

## Exam 6: Nature

1. A B C D
2. A B C D
3. A B C D
4. A B C D
5. A B C D
6. A B C D
7. A B C D
8. A B C D
9. A B C D
10. A B C D
11. A B C D
12. A B C D
13. A B C D
14. A B C D
15. A B C D
16. A B C D
17. A B C D
18. A B C D
19. A B C D
20. A B C D
21. A B C D
22. A B C D
23. A B C D
24. A B C D
25. A B C D
26. A B C D
27. A B C D
28. A B C D
29. A B C D
30. A B C D
31. A B C D
32. A B C D
33. A B C D
34. A B C D
35. A B C D

## Exam 7: History

1. A B C D
2. A B C D
3. A B C D
4. A B C D
5. A B C D
6. A B C D
7. A B C D
8. A B C D
9. A B C D
10. A B C D
11. A B C D
12. A B C D
13. A B C D
14. A B C D
15. A B C D
16. A B C D
17. A B C D
18. A B C D
19. A B C D

## Exam 8: Fun & Games

1. A B C D
2. A B C D
3. A B C D
4. A B C D
5. A B C D
6. A B C D
7. A B C D
8. A B C D
9. A B C D
10. A B C D
11. A B C D
12. A B C D
13. A B C D
14. A B C D
15. A B C D
16. A B C D
17. A B C D
18. A B C D
19. A B C D
20. A B C D
21. A B C D
22. A B C D
23. A B C D
24. A B C D
25. A B C D
26. A B C D
27. A B C D
28. A B C D
29. A B C D
30. A B C D
31. A B C D
32. A B C D

# Answer Sheet

## Exam 1: Geography

1. B
2. A
3. D
4. C
5. A
6. A
7. C
8. C
9. A
10. B
11. B
12. A
13. D
14. B
15. D
16. C
17. D
18. A
19. B
20. D
21. B
22. A
23. A
24. B
25. D
26. C
27. A
28. C
29. C
30. B
31. D
32. C
33. A
34. C
35. B
36. B
37. D
38. A
39. C
40. B
41. D
42. C
43. D
44. A
45. B
46. D
47. B
48. A
49. D
50. B

## Exam 2: Music

1. A
2. D
3. C
4. C
5. B
6. B
7. B
8. B
9. C
10. B
11. B
12. A
13. A
14. C
15. C
16. B
17. B
18. B
19. B
20. C
21. D
22. D
23. D
24. A
25. B
26. C
27. A
28. A
29. C
30. B
31. C
32. B
33. C
34. A
35. C
36. D
37. B
38. A

## Exam 3: Human

1. D
2. C
3. C
4. C
5. D
6. D
7. C
8. A
9. C
10. A
11. B
12. B
13. B
14. C
15. A
16. A
17. D
18. A
19. B
20. D
21. A
22. B
23. A
24. A
25. B
26. A
27. D
28. A
29. B
30. B
31. B
32. A
33. B
34. A
35. B
36. D
37. B

## Exam 4: Space

1. D
2. A
3. D
4. B
5. B
6. A
7. B
8. B
9. A
10. A
11. A
12. D
13. D
14. A
15. B
16. A
17. B
18. D
19. B
20. D
21. B
22. B
23. A
24. A
25. A
26. A
27. B
28. A
29. B
30. C
31. A
32. C
33. A
34. D
35. A
36. B
37. C

## Exam 5: Art

1. C
2. C
3. B
4. A
5. C
6. A
7. C
8. A
9. B
10. A
11. B
12. C
13. C
14. A
15. C
16. B
17. B
18. D
19. B
20. D
21. A
22. B
23. B
24. D
25. A
26. C
27. C
28. D
29. A
30. B
31. B
32. C
33. C
34. C
35. A

## Exam 6: Nature

1. B
2. A
3. D
4. B
5. A
6. A
7. B
8. C
9. B
10. B
11. C
12. C
13. C
14. D
15. C
16. B
17. C
18. C
19. C
20. B
21. C
22. B
23. B
24. A
25. A
26. A
27. C
28. D
29. B
30. B
31. A
32. C
33. D
34. B
35. C

## Exam 7: History

1. A
2. C
3. A
4. B
5. B
6. B
7. A
8. A
9. C
10. C
11. D
12. C
13. A
14. B
15. A
16. C
17. A
18. C
19. B
20. B
21. A
22. C
23. A
24. D
25. C
26. B
27. C
28. B
29. C
30. C
31. B
32. C
33. C
34. B
35. C

## Exam 8: Fun & Games

1. C
2. B
3. B
4. C
5. C
6. C
7. A
8. D
9. D
10. B
11. B
12. C
13. C
14. A
15. B
16. A
17. A
18. A
19. B
20. B
21. B
22. C
23. A
24. D
25. D
26. B
27. C
28. D
29. C
30. C
31. D
32. A